THE FINAL
HOPE

THREE MESSAGES FOR AN ANXIOUS WORLD

CLIFFORD GOLDSTEIN

REVIEW AND HERALD® PUBLISHING ASSOCIATION
Since 1861 | www.reviewandherald.com

This book was
Copyedited by: James Cavil
Cover designed by: Viviene Martinelli
Cover art by: Shaiith/Shutterstock
Desktop layout by: Melinda Worden
Typeset: Minion Pro 10/12

PRINTED IN INDIA.

ISBN 978-1-78665-148-8

To order, call +44(0)1476 591700 or email *sales@stanboroughpress.org.uk*.
Visit us at *www.stanboroughpress.org.uk* for information on our other products.

CONTENTS

CONTENTS ...

Section One

The Big Freeze, Crunch, Rip

For years Hollywood has cranked out film after film about the end of the world, or at least the end of the world as we now know it. *Armageddon* (1998), *Zombieland* (2009), *Mad Max: Fury Road* (2015), *This Is the End* (2013), *Greenland* (2020), just to name a few, depict a pretty sorry future for us all. And suddenly, with COVID-19 (including variants, such as B.1.1.7 or B.1.351 and counting) Hollywood's science fiction end-of-the-world stuff seems a little too close to home for comfort.

Science fiction aside, real science presents a future that is, to put it mildly, rather bleak as well. Sooner or later the universe, scientists say—not just the earth, but the *universe!*—is going to end. How? Depending upon the numbers that these scientists stick in their physics equations, some theorize that the universe might tear itself apart (the Big Rip). Others, using different numbers, predict that it might collapse in on itself (the Big Crunch). The most popular scenario is that it might burn out (the Big Freeze): "The universe," wrote Paul Davies, "currently aglow with the prolific energy of nuclear power, will eventually exhaust this valuable resource. The era of light will be forever over."[1]

Big Crunch, Big Rip, Big Freeze—long-term, things don't look very hopeful for this world, do they?

Interestingly enough, the Bible depicts the end of this world as well, just quite differently than either Hollywood or science do. A few biblical excerpts about our long-term prospects: "For behold, I create new heavens and a new earth; and the former shall not be remembered or come to mind" (Isaiah 65:17). "Nevertheless we, according to His promise, look for new heavens and a new earth in which righteousness

[1] Paul Davies, *The Last Three Minutes* (New York: BasicBooks, 1994), pp. 49, 50.

dwells" (2 Peter 3:13). "Now I saw a new heaven and a new earth, for the first heaven and the first earth had passed away. Also, there was no more sea. Then I, John, saw the holy city, New Jerusalem, coming down out of heaven from God, prepared as a bride adorned for her husband" (Revelation 21:1, 2). Or this, one of the most hopeful: "And God will wipe away every tear from their eyes; there shall be no more death, nor sorrow, nor crying. There shall be no more pain, for the former things have passed away" (verse 4).

Not quite the Big Freeze or the Big Crunch, is it? Nor the future depicted in *Zombieland*, either.

Yes, both science and biblical revelation agree: our world as it is will not remain this way forever. Everything will change. But what about us and our loved ones? Is the end of the world the ultimate end of us all as well? The Big Rip, the Big Freeze—none of these options offer us any long-term hope, do they?

No. They offer us nothing but the prospect that we and our loved ones—and, in fact, every person who has ever lived or will live—will vanish into eternal oblivion. The obvious conclusion of all is that we, ultimately, mean nothing, and that our lives mean nothing, and that we are of no more significance than a cloud of cosmic dust. "Must I again declare to you the supreme vacuity of culture, of science, of art, of good, of truth, of beauty, of justice," wrote Spain's Miguel de Unamuno, ". . . of all these beautiful conceptions, if at the last, in four days or in four million of centuries—it matters not which—no human consciousness shall exist to appropriate this civilization, this science, art, good, truth, beauty, justice, and all the rest?"[2]

The Bible, in contrast, presents the promise of a radically different future for the world and, most important, for us: a new heaven and a new earth. However, this promise of a new heaven and a new earth leads to the logical question: What happened to the old heavens and the old earth? What happens to them, and to us—we who live under and on them? The answer is full of hope and promise. They, the old heavens, the old earth, are going to be swept away, replaced by a new heaven and a new earth, which will be inhabited by people for eternity in an existence without sin, suffering, sickness, and death. A concept

---

[2] Miguel de Unamuno, *Tragic Sense of Life* (New York: Dover Publications, 1954), p. 96.

hard to imagine for beings like us, who have known only sin, suffering, sickness, and death.

However, Scripture says that before all this happens, a terrible crisis will be unleashed upon the world—a crisis that will make some of these Hollywood end-of-the-world flicks look tame. The Old Testament prophet Daniel warned: "And there shall be a time of trouble, such as never was since there was a nation, even to that time" (Daniel 12:1). And who, since the COVID-19 outbreak, doubts that the whole world can, overnight, face a crisis? And who doesn't sense that this COVID crisis might be only the beginning of woes, and that something worse could await us?

According to the Bible, something worse does.

The good news, however, is that God, who "so loved the world that He gave His only begotten Son, that whoever believes in Him should not perish but have everlasting life" (John 3:16)—this same God has not left us without a hope, without a warning, without a way of escape, if not from the trials, at least from the hopeless despair and destruction these last-day trials will bring for way too many.

From the beginning to the end of the Bible, the prophets, though they themselves had faced everything—sickness, depression, war, natural disasters, prison, exile, torture, death—that the fallen world could throw at them, could nevertheless write again and again about the love and goodness of God. Isaiah, 2,500 years ago, penned: "'Though the mountains be shaken and the hills be removed, yet my unfailing love for you will not be shaken nor my covenant of peace be removed,' says the Lord, who has compassion on you" (Isaiah 54:10, NIV). The psalmist, almost 3,000 years ago, could sing: "Give thanks to the God of heaven. His love endures forever" (Psalm 136:26, NIV). The apostle Paul, who experienced prison, physical ailments, hatred, mob violence, poverty, hunger, cold, could write—in a world almost 2,000 years away from anaesthetics—that "God demonstrates his own love for us in this: While we were still sinners, Christ died for us" (Romans 5:8, NIV).

In other words, though some people try to use the evil in this world as an excuse to reject the existence of God, or certainly the existence of a loving God, the Bible writers didn't, couldn't, because they knew the Lord and they knew for themselves His love. And one manifestation of His love is seen when God warns His people about what is coming, so that they can be prepared for it. And if He would do that for ancient Israel and Judah (so much of the prophetic writings are the prophets warning those two nations about what was coming), relatively small kingdoms compared to the world, how much more so would He give the whole world itself a warning, a chance to be prepared for what is coming, for "a time of trouble, such as never was since there was a nation, even to that time"?

And He has. That warning is found in the book of Revelation, the last book of the Bible, in what are known as the three angels' messages of Revelation 14. Who are these angels? What are these messages? What warning do they give to a world obviously in trouble? And most important, what hope do they (as opposed to, for example, the Big Freeze or any of the other hopeless alternatives that, we're told, await us) offer us for the long-term, eternal future?

Principalities and Powers

Who, outside on a cloudless night (away from city lights) and staring at the stars fiercely burning against the cosmos, hasn't been awed? Especially by the sheer number? But even on the clearest night, when we can see more stars than we can count before the morning sun washes them away, what are we seeing in contrast to what's out there? Please! Less than a drop in an ocean of water.

It's estimated that there could be as many as 2 trillion galaxies hurling through the creation. *Trillion.* And counting. Each galaxy has an average of about 100 billion stars. One hundred billion multiplied by 2 trillion add up to a lot of stars. And astronomers are now discovering what they call "exoplanets." These are planets that orbit their stars the way the planets in our solar system do the sun, our star. According to NASA, about 4,000 exoplanets have been discovered.[3] That's all that they can see, at least for now. If the number of exoplanets is anywhere near the number of stars, or galaxies even (that is, only one exoplanet *per galaxy*?)—the universe is filled with more planets than we can imagine.

Which means what? That the odds are that we are not alone in

---

[3] https://exoplanets.nasa.gov/faq/6/how-many-exoplanets-are-there/

the universe, and that other life exists in the creation. There's even an organization, first started by NASA, called SETI, the Search for Extraterrestrial Intelligence, dedicated to discovering life in another part of the creation besides earth.

The irony is that while the diligent and faithful seekers at SETI have been aiming their fancy devices into the sky, hoping for a cosmic Tweet or whatever from another part of the creation, the Bible, written thousands of years ago, not only talks about the existence of "extraterrestrial" life but also gives us some insights into the moral character of that life, at least some of it. That is, the Bible tells us what common sense tells us: in all this vast universe, we are not alone.

What follows are a few scriptural excerpts about life existing in other parts of the creation:

"His intent was that now, through the church, the manifold wisdom of God should be made known to the rulers and authorities in the heavenly realms" (Ephesians 3:10, NIV). Rulers and authorities . . . where? In heavenly realms—that is, in another part of the creation other than the earth. Even more fascinating is that according to this text, these rulers and authorities learn about God from what happens here on earth with God's church.

Another text: "For our struggle is not against flesh and blood, but against the rulers, against the powers, against the world rulers of this darkness, against the spiritual forces of evil in the heavens" (Ephesians 6:12, NET). Wow! This is an insight that SETI, so far, hasn't come close to uncovering. The text talks about "our struggle." Against whom? The spiritual forces of evil in the heavens, that's whom. The implications of this verse, along with the others, are stunning. Not only does other life in the universe exist, but some of it is evil. And that evil is working against us on earth.

Another biblical text: "For in him all things were created: things in heaven and on earth, visible and invisible, whether thrones or powers or rulers or authorities; all things have been created through him and for him" (Colossians 1:16, NIV). Here the Bible is talking about Jesus as the Creator of all things (see John 1:1-3) in both the heavens and the earth, "visible and invisible," including "thrones or powers or rulers or authorities."

Some texts in the book of Revelation flesh out this idea more: "And war broke out in heaven: Michael and his angels fought with the dragon; and the dragon and his angels fought, but they did not prevail, nor was a place found for them in heaven any longer. So the great dragon was cast out, that serpent of old, called the Devil and Satan, who deceives the whole world; he was cast to the earth, and his angels were cast out with him. . . . Therefore rejoice, O heavens, and you who dwell in them! Woe to the inhabitants of the earth and the sea! For the devil has come down to you, having great wrath, because he knows that he has a short time" (Revelation 12:7-12).

What is the Bible saying? First, we are not alone in the cosmos. Other intelligent life exists out there, which, again, considering all size of the cosmos and all the stars in it, shouldn't be surprising. It would be surprising if there *weren't* other life out there. Second, some of this life is hostile, is evil, and has brought their evil to this earth. If "war broke out in heaven," and some of the combatants are here, any wonder that there's so much strife on earth as well? What these verses, and others like them, reveal is what has been called the great controversy theme, a controversy between good and evil that, though beginning in another part of the creation, is being played out here on earth.

And really—who needs divine revelation to see, if not the source of this great controversy, its reality? Many people, secular or religious, even if they don't know the details or origins of it, can sense the battle between good and evil in our world.

The poet T. S. Eliot wrote:

"The world turns and the world changes,
But one thing does not change.
In all of my years, one thing does not change,
However you disguise it, this thing does not change:
The perpetual struggle of Good and Evil."[4]

Even a harsh atheist like German Friedrich Nietzsche wrote: "Let us conclude. The two opposing values 'good and bad,' 'good and evil,'

---

[4] From T. S. Eliot, *The Rock*, https://books.apple.com/us/book/the-rock/id837916987.

have been engaged in a fearful struggle on earth for thousands of years; and though the latter value has certainly been on top for a long time, there are still places where the struggle is as yet undecided."[5]

One theologian, Michael Brown, talking about the struggle between good and evil, called it a "cosmic conflict."[6] Another, John Peckham, has written a book on the subject called *Theodicy of Love: Cosmic Conflict and the Problem of Evil.*[7]

What is a *theodicy*? It's an attempt to answer the question that everyone who believed in a loving God asks: Why, if God is so good, and so loving, and so powerful, is there so much evil in the world? And, as we will see, the three angels' messages are central to answering that question, perhaps the most important one that anyone could ask.

The Risk of Love

Unless you've had a bad experience with a dog, most people love them. They are, after all, friendly, affectionate, faithful, loyal, and, to the degree that a dog can express emotion, loving. Their wagging tails, often in excitement to see you, make them delightful companions. In fact, some dogs, called service dogs, are used to help people with emotional problems. That's how soothing and comforting dogs can be. And who doesn't like petting them?

Of course, dogs can also be trouble. They can bite, soil the carpet, get sick, chew furniture, shed, and cost money to keep healthy and to feed. All dog owners, even the most passionate ones, have had moments when they thought, *Is a dog really worth the bother?*

Suppose, however, you could have a dog that never soiled the carpet, never got sick, never bit anyone, and cost no money to keep healthy? Who wouldn't jump at getting a dog like that? You can. How about Sony's AIBO, for instance? What is AIBO? It means "companion" in Japanese, and according to Sony, AIBO "is a true companion with real emotions and instincts. With loving attention from his master, he will develop into a more mature and fun-loving friend as time passes."

[5] Friedrich Nietzsche, *The Genealogy of Morals* (1887), p. 16.

[6] Michael Brown, *Job: The Faith to Challenge God* (Peabody, Mass.: Hendrickson Publishers, 2019), p. 30.

[7] John C. Peckham, *Theodicy of Love: Cosmic Conflict and the Problem of Evil,* Kindle edition (Grand Rapids: Baker Publishing Group, 2018), p. 4.

What is Sony talking about? A robot dog.

A robot?

"AIBO actually has emotions and instincts programmed into his brain," says SONY about its dog. "He acts to fulfill the desires created by his instincts. If satisfied, his joy level will rise. If not, then he will get sad or angry. Like any living being, AIBO learns how to get what he wants. Occasionally he will wave his legs around vigorously or show signs of anger if he does not receive the kind of attention he requests from you. The way you respond to his emotional expressions greatly influences his personality and growth. . . . Even though AIBO is made from plastic, powered by a battery, and has a nervous system of integrated circuitry, he is also a fully cognizant, sensing, loving, and communicative companion."[8]

Emotions? Instincts? Desires? Talk about false advertising! Robot dogs have no more emotions, instincts, and desires than does your kitchen sink. To claim that AIBO is "also a fully cognizant, sensing, loving, and communicative companion" is to attribute traits of intelligent life to plastic and metal. We barely understand how living tissue, brain cells, can house (create, facilitate, whatever) emotions and desires, yet we're supposed to believe that Sony had produced a robot dog (a dog?) that manifests love and joy and happiness? Just make sure that the batteries are charged, and love, joy, and affection will flow out of the circuit boards, silicon chips, and plastic like photons from a light source. The whole idea is ridiculous. To mistake a computerized dog wagging a tail as an expression of happiness would be like attributing moral integrity to the zeroes and ones in a software program that filters out child porn.

If the idea of a robot dog showing "affection" and "love" leaves you cold, and if you would not want AIBO to replace your flesh-and-blood pet, even with all its potential problems—then you understand the heart and soul of the great controversy. Instead of creating beings (either in the heavens, such as angels, or on the earth, such as humans) like robots, God created them with the ability to love. Rather than robots, He created us as moral beings with the capacity to love both Him and others, and this moral capacity included freedom, the

---

[8] http://www.robotbooks.com/sony_aibo.htm

freedom inherent in the kind of love that only a free being could give. Love that is forced is not love; if God wanted beings who could love, He had to create them free, truly free.

And freedom, true freedom, entails risks. For example, the Bible talks about the abuse of this freedom by an angel called Lucifer. It says:

"You were the anointed cherub who covers;

I established you;

You were on the holy mountain of God;

You walked back and forth in the midst of fiery stones.

You were perfect in your ways from the day you were created,

Till iniquity was found in you" (Ezekiel 28:14, 15).

This was a heavenly being, an angel created by God. And how did God create him? "You were perfect in your ways from the day you were created." *Perfect?* And yet, what happened to this perfect being? "Iniquity was found in you." Iniquity found in a being made "perfect" by God? How could this be? It's easy: this perfection included freedom, moral freedom, and Lucifer violated that freedom.

It's the same principle here. Genesis 1-2 revealed God creating life on earth, which concluded with Adam and Eve, both made in God's image. "So God created man in His own image; in the image of God He created him; male and female He created them" (Genesis 1:27). And when the creation was done, God Himself declared it "very good" (verse 31).

So we have perfect beings (surely, having been made in God's image, they were as "perfect" as Lucifer had been) created by a perfect God on a perfect earth. And yet, what happened? Genesis 3 reveals, through the trickery of "the serpent" (verses 1-6) that these perfect beings fell into sin. How could that happen? Because being perfect included the ability to love, and love demanded freedom, and freedom includes risk.

In this context, the following texts become clearer: "And war broke out in heaven: Michael and his angels fought with the dragon; and the dragon and his angels fought, but they did not prevail, nor was a place found for them in heaven any longer. So the great dragon was cast out, that serpent of old, called the Devil and Satan, who deceives the whole world; he was cast to the earth, and his angels were cast out with him" (Revelation 12:7-9).

Evil, rebellion, war—all these began in heaven, in God's perfect heaven, with the fall of Lucifer. Next, Lucifer, now called "the Devil and Satan," came to the earth, and here he, "the serpent of old" (see Genesis 3:1-6), brought his rebellion. In short, though the great controversy started in another part of the universe, it is being played out on the earth.

Couldn't God, however, have stopped all this from happening from the start?

How?

First, He could have created humans without the capacity to love. He could have made a race of robots who, whatever else they did, would not, could not, love. But God wanted a relationship of love between Him and humans, and had He made us like robots, there would have been none. We couldn't love Him back any more than a toaster can love its owner; any relationship would have been no deeper than one has with a toaster.

Second, He could have wiped out Lucifer the moment he started his rebellion. *Zap!* However, that option doesn't work either. Suppose you were a loving, caring leader of a people. Then, for some unfair and unjust reason, someone started a rebellion, accusing you of being vicious, selfish, arbitrary, and dictatorial. In response, even before a trial, before letting them argue their case before you and others— you just lined them up against a wall and shot them. You might have quelled the rebellion, yes. But what about the charges made against you? Your actions would have proved their exact charges: that you were, in fact, vicious, selfish, arbitrary, and dictatorial. If you were a vicious leader who ruled by fear, by threats, you would simply scare them into obedience.

But Scripture teaches that God is a God of love, and He operates out of love, not fear. "And we have known and believed the love that God has for us. God is love, and he who abides in love abides in God, and God in him" (1 John 4:16). When asked what the most important commandment was, Jesus answered, " 'And you shall love the Lord your God with all your heart, with all your soul, with all your mind, and with all your strength.' This is the first commandment" (Mark 12:30). God can command us to love Him; He just can't force us to. To love Him, we have to do it freely.

So then, without violating the principle of love, how is a God of love going to solve the great controversy? Imagine the leader who was accused by rebels of being vicious, selfish, arbitrary, and dictatorial. Suppose this leader, though still their leader, voluntarily came down to the level of his people, lived among them, suffered among them, and even sacrificed his life for them, showing that the charges against him, that he was vicious, selfish, arbitrary, and dictatorial, were the opposite of what he was like. In fact, what if the very ones who made the charges against him were the very ones who had him killed, proving that they themselves were guilty of the things that they accused the leader of being?

Though only an analogy, in a very general way this is the big picture of Jesus Christ, Jesus of Nazareth, on the cross. God in the flesh answered the charges of Satan. Christ, though the Creator (see John 1:13), took upon Himself humanity, and in that humanity revealed to angels, and to the world, what God was really like. Though the great controversy continues, as Satan is still in rebellion, his demise is certain. "Therefore rejoice, O heavens, and you who dwell in them! Woe to the inhabitants of the earth and the sea! For the devil has come down to you, having great wrath, because he knows that he has a short time" (Revelation 12:12).

And the revelation of the character of God, the self-denying, self-renouncing character of God, as revealed at the cross—here is the foundation of three angels' messages, messages of hope, of promise, and of eternal life offered to a world that's heading toward dissolution. The promise is there for all of us, and each one of us—having the freedom inherent in love—has to choose to claim what has been so graciously offered in Jesus.

The Revelation of Jesus Christ

What are the three angels' messages? They read as follows:

"Then I saw another angel flying in the midst of heaven, having the everlasting gospel to preach to those who dwell on the earth—to every nation, tribe, tongue, and people—saying with a loud voice, 'Fear God and give glory to Him, for the hour of His judgment has come;

and worship Him who made heaven and earth, the sea and springs of water.' And another angel followed, saying, 'Babylon is fallen, is fallen, that great city, because she has made all nations drink of the wine of the wrath of her fornication.' Then a third angel followed them, saying with a loud voice, 'If anyone worships the beast and his image, and receives his mark on his forehead or on his hand, he himself shall also drink of the wine of the wrath of God, which is poured out full strength into the cup of His indignation. He shall be tormented with fire and brimstone in the presence of the holy angels and in the presence of the Lamb. And the smoke of their torment ascends forever and ever; and they have no rest day or night, who worship the beast and his image, and whoever receives the mark of his name.' Here is the patience of the saints; here are those who keep the commandments of God and the faith of Jesus" (Revelation 14:6-12).

That's it. About 220 words in the New King James Version. And yet in these nouns and verbs and prepositions are "mysteries" (1 Corinthians 4:1), deep things that "angels desire to look into" (1 Peter 1:12) but have now been revealed to us. The three angels' messages are expressions of truths that God had established, not just "before the foundation of the world" (Ephesians 1:4), but "before time began" (2 Timothy 1:9)—a long time ago! Embedded in these texts about specific, earthly things—i.e., nations, people, springs of water, and the beast—are eternal truths that existed before even time did and will remain throughout eternity.

The messages appear in the book of Revelation, the last book in the Christian Bible, which makes sense because the book is about last-day events. The fancy theological word is "eschatology," the study of final events. Just as the book of Genesis, the first book of the Bible, dealt with the creation of the world and the first events in it, Revelation, the last book of the Bible, deals with last events in it, leading up to the end of this world and the creation of a new one, "a new heaven and a new earth" (Revelation 21:1).

The word "Revelation" appears in the first line of the book: "The Revelation of Jesus Christ, which God gave Him to show His servants—things which must shortly take place" (Revelation 1:1). The word for "revelation" in Greek, *apokalypsis*, means an "uncovering" or a "revealing," from which we get the word "revelation."

And it is a revelation of what? The "revelation of Jesus Christ." That is, the book teaches us about Jesus, about who He is: "I am the Alpha and the Omega, the Beginning and the End" (Revelation 1:8), the eternal God; and yet it also depicts Him as "the Lamb slain from the foundation of the world" (Revelation 13:8), the crucified Savior, the one who died on the cross, slain for the sins of the world.

Though Revelation is a New Testament book, just like the rest of the New Testament it relies heavily on the Old. Scholar Ranko Stefanovic argues of the 404 verses in Revelation, 278 refer or allude to the Old Testament, including such key events as the Creation, the Flood, and the Exodus. No other New Testament book relies so heavily on the Old.

This point becomes very important in seeking to understand the meaning of Revelation, including the three angels' messages. Many of its words and phrases—i.e., "Babylon," "the beast," "the commandments of God," "the wine of wrath," "forever and ever"—cannot be properly understood apart from how they are used in the Old Testament. In fact, the Old Testament is the key to unlocking the important truths given in this, the final book of the Bible, with its message for those living in these hard days of earth's tragic history.

A Bit of Context, Please (Part One)

The book of Revelation, written by the apostle John when he had been exiled to an island, Patmos, off the coast of modern Turkey, covers Christian history, basically from the time of Jesus through the end of our world and the creation of a new one. The book has 22 chapters, with the three angels' messages appearing in chapter 14, a little more than halfway through Revelation.

To best understand the messages, one needs a bit of the context in which they appear. A quick summary of the two preceding chapters, 12 and 13, creates that context.

Revelation 12, like much of Revelation, doesn't appear in a strict chronological order. It jumps back and forth between events, even though a basic flow, a progression, of Christian history does unfold all through the book of Revelation. That is why, for instance, by the time we get to the last chapters of Revelation, the emphasis is on the redeemed living in a new heaven and a new earth, even though there are flashbacks to previous events.

We read earlier from Revelation 12, with the depiction of the war in heaven (verse 7) and the casting to the earth of Satan and his angels. In other words, central to everything is the great controversy scenario, which appears all through the chapter. This controversy started, as we have seen, in heaven. Next, the controversy comes to earth, when the dragon (Satan) seeks to devour a child (Jesus), "the moment he was born" (verse 4, NIV). This happened when Satan, using King Herod, tried to have the infant Jesus killed. Indeed, an angel told Joseph, Mary's husband, "Arise, take the young Child and His mother, flee to Egypt, and stay there until I bring you word; for Herod will seek the young Child to destroy Him" (Matthew 2:13).

However, just as Satan and his angels failed in their war in heaven—they were, after all, cast out (Revelation 9)—they failed also in trying to destroy the infant Jesus. Eventually Jesus, while on earth, defeated Satan at the cross. Having "disarmed principalities and powers, He made a public spectacle of them, triumphing over them in it" (Colossians 2:15). In fact, Jesus rose from death, so that "through death He might destroy him who had the power of death, that is, the devil" (Hebrews 2:14).

Revelation 12 depicts Christ's next victory over Satan like this. "And her Child was caught up to God and His throne" (verse 5). That is, after the cross, Jesus ascended to heaven, where He ministers in our behalf in heaven (see Hebrews 7-10).

Defeated in heaven by Jesus, defeated at the cross by Jesus, Satan still had not given up in his attack on Christ's people. All through the Bible God's church has been symbolized by a woman, or even a pure bride (2 Corinthians 11:2; Jeremiah 2:2). After the cross, Satan is depicted in Revelation 12 as persecuting God's church, symbolized by a woman:

"Now when the dragon saw that he had been cast to the earth, he persecuted the woman who gave birth to the male Child. But the woman was given two wings of a great eagle, that she might fly into the wilderness to her place, where she is nourished for a time and times and half a time, from the presence of the serpent. So the serpent spewed water out of his mouth like a flood after the woman, that he might cause her to be carried away by the flood. But the earth helped the woman, and the earth opened its mouth and swallowed up the flood which the dragon had spewed out of his mouth" (verses 13-16).

Again, we're seeing here symbolism, the kind found all through Revelation: a dragon, a serpent spewing water, the earth opening its mouth, and so forth. Here, too, even amid the symbolism, the great controversy motif prevails, with Satan trying, and yet failing, to destroy the woman, God's church. For example, the woman fleeing into the "wilderness" is an allusion to ancient Israel living in the wilderness, during which God protected it from its enemies and from destruction (see Psalm 78:52)—another example of how the Old Testament holds the key to interpreting Revelation.

Historically, after Jesus ascended to heaven, the Christian church faced persecution, sometimes massive, from Rome. Who hasn't heard stories of Christians being fed to the lions or burned alive as torches in the Roman Colosseum? Starting with Nero, in A.D. 64, the Romans attacked Christians in various ways, and with various degrees of intensity, over the next few centuries. Accused of most dreadful crimes, Christians were declared to be the cause of many of the calamities— famine, pestilence, earthquakes—that ravaged the empire. They were condemned as rebels against Rome and its empire, as foes of religion, and as detrimental to society. One ancient historian described the persecution of Christians in Rome this way:

"Christus [Christ], from whom the name had its origin, suffered the extreme penalty during the reign of Tiberius at the hands of one of our procurators, Pontius Pilate, and a most mischievous superstition, thus checked for the moment, again broke out not only in Judaea, the first source of the evil, but even in Rome, where all things hideous and shameful from every part of the world find their center and become popular.

"Accordingly, an arrest was first made of all who pleaded guilty; then, upon their information, an immense multitude was convicted, not so much of the crime of firing the city, as of hatred against mankind. Mockery of every sort was added to their deaths. Covered with the skins of beasts, they were torn by dogs and perished, or were nailed to crosses, or were doomed to the flames and burnt, to serve as a nightly illumination, when daylight had expired."[9]

Unfortunately, history shows, too, that even after the Roman Empire became "Christianized," the persecution didn't stop. Under the tutelage of the popes, Rome continued the persecution of those who didn't follow its man-made rules and traditions. This, too, went on in various degrees for more than 1,000 years, becoming particularly ferocious during the time of the Reformation, and ending only when secular forces began to dominate Europe, seen in something like the capture in 1798 of the pope by a French general in the aftermath of the French Revolution. Revelation 12, using broad symbols, depicted this history, this attempt by Satan to destroy God's church.

However, the great controversy continues, as seen in the last verse of the chapter: "And the dragon was wroth with the woman, and went to make war with the remnant of her seed, which keep the commandments of God, and have the testimony of Jesus Christ" (Revelation 12:17, KJV).

The dragon, Satan, "enraged" with the woman, God's church, whom he failed to destroy, now "went to make war with the remnant of her seed." That is, even after the centuries of persecution, God still has people, faithful people, who are the subject of Satan's wrath—and they are depicted as those who "keep the commandments of God, and have the testimony of Jesus Christ."

A Bit of Context, Please (Part Two)

Revelation 13, like Revelation 12, continues the great controversy motif. Even without understanding the precise meaning of the symbols, one can see the dragon (Revelation 13:2, 4, 11), Satan, attempt to wreak havoc here on earth. The early verses, using imagery from Daniel 7 (again, more evidence of how the book of Revelation is heavily tied to the Old Testament), recount the history of church persecution through the Dark Ages.

However, a point worth remembering, especially amid the depiction of persecution and suffering that follows, is that by now in the

---

[9] https://www.livius.org/sources/content/tacitus/tacitus-on-the-christians/

great controversy, Satan (the dragon, the serpent) has already been beaten three times by Christ: defeated in heaven (Revelation 12:8), defeated at the cross (Colossians 2:15), and finally, defeated in his attempts to destroy Christ's church, because a remnant of His people have survived (Revelation 12:17). In short, as long as one stays connected to Christ, one is always on the winning side in the great controversy.

But it doesn't mean that times won't be hard. Just as the early church over the centuries faced persecution, Revelation 13 talks about more persecution, future persecution on a worldwide scale. And if the COVID-19 pandemic has taught us anything, it's about how quickly the whole world can be brought to heel, how the whole world can suddenly, dramatically, and in unexpected ways, change—and not for the good, either.

Revelation 13 depicts what's coming like this: "All who dwell on the earth will worship him, whose names have not been written in the Book of Life of the Lamb slain from the foundation of the world. . . . He was granted power to give breath to the image of the beast, that the image of the beast should both speak and cause as many as would not worship the image of the beast to be killed. He causes all, both small and great, rich and poor, free and slave, to receive a mark on their right hand or on their foreheads, and that no one may buy or sell except one who has the mark or the name of the beast, or the number of his name" (Revelation 13:8-17).

Over the years all sorts of popular books and movies have come out about who these powers are and how all these events will be made manifest. Each book, each movie, however, tells a different story, with all sorts of wild speculation. If we put aside, for now, an attempt to explain what these verses, rich in Old Testament symbolism, mean, a few points come through that are important for understanding what is going on here and that can help us better understand the three angels' messages.

First, as we have already seen, this persecution is worldwide. Which makes sense in that, as shown in Revelation 12, when Satan was cast to the earth, his attempts at deception were universal: "So the great dragon was cast out, that serpent of old, called the Devil and Satan, who deceives *the whole world*; he was cast to the earth, and his angels were cast out with him" (verse 9). And again, not to belabor the point, after COVID-19 who can deny how the world can quickly be changed and brought into turmoil and trial? It would be the height of folly to deny that what is depicted here could happen, not after what "the whole world" has been facing since 2020.

Second, a key theme appears in these verses: *worship*. Five times (Revelation 13:4 [twice], 8, 12, 15) worship is shown to be a major factor behind the turmoil and conflict depicted in the last days. According to these verses, the dragon, Satan, will attempt to enforce a certain kind of worship upon the world. In one sense this shouldn't be surprising, because, from the beginning of the great controversy, Satan has wanted to usurp the authority and place of God Himself. An Old Testament depiction of his attitude has been revealed in these verses: "For you have said in your heart: 'I will ascend into heaven. I will exalt my throne above the stars of God; I will also sit on the mount of the congregation on the farthest sides of the north; I will ascend above the heights of the clouds, I will be like the Most High'" (Isaiah 14:13, 14). This point, that about worship and whom people worship, becomes paramount in understanding the three angels' messages.

Third, in stark contrast to God, who seeks worship and obedience only by love and the freedom inherent in love, the forces of evil will use violence, as well as economic pressure, to enforce worship. The texts says that they will "cause as many as would not worship the image of the beast to be killed" (Revelation 13:15), and that "no one may buy or sell" (verse 17) unless they conform.

In short, Revelation 12-13 provide the context for the three angels' messages, which follow. Unfortunately, the context, that of worldwide religious persecution, is not a pretty one, not a hopeful one, in and of itself. However, the great news of the three angels' messages is that they reveal where our hope is, where our promise. And amid this coming time of confusion, turmoil, and persecution (in some ways the great controversy climaxing on the earth), the Lord offers everyone hope and promise, which, even now, before this persecution has arisen, we can all surely use, can't we?

And though the context of the following verse is different, the sentiment behind them remains an eternal principle, one that each one of us can draw comfort from. "For I know the thoughts that I think toward you, says the Lord, thoughts of peace and not of evil, to give you a future and a hope" (Jeremiah 29:11). And the Lord has proved the truthfulness of that sentiment by the death of Jesus, which offers everyone who claims it "a future and a hope." And that future, and that hope, are revealed in the three angels' messages.

Section Two

Human Angels

Ever hear of Helen Keller? She was an American woman born in 1880 who, through a very early illness, lost her sight and hearing. Nevertheless, she graduated college, wrote books, and traveled the world advocating for the rights of those with disabilities like hers. Though two crucial avenues for communication were lost, she was still able to communicate with others and others with her.

From the cells in our body that communicate with other cells, to plants that communicate with other plants (sending chemicals in the air), to animals that communicate with other animals, and humans, whose civilizations are built upon communication—life is communication. We need to talk, to listen, to speak, to hear, and even those who can't speak or hear can and do still communicate. And, please, in the day and age of smartphones, which provide a means of communication that a generation ago would have seemed straight out of science fiction, our existence today, perhaps more than ever, is built upon communication. We live in what has been called the information age. And what good is information if it is not communicated, not shared?

Thus, the very name, the three angels' messages—*messages*—implies something to be communicated, to be taught, to be revealed, and because they come from the Bible, the Word of God, we can trust what they say as true. After all, who hasn't learned by now that with the tools of mass communication literally in our hands, not all that's taught and communicated is truth. Just as a math problem can have one right answer and an infinite number of wrong ones, how much of what pops up on digital screens is true or, in fact, even worth our time and energy reading and listening to? For every truth out there, only God knows how many lies circle it like vultures.

Amid all the misinformation, the book of Revelation early on tells us, "Blessed is he who reads and those who hear the words of this prophecy, and keep those things which are written in it; for the time is near" (Revelation 1:3). God is communicating with us through His Word, and we're blessed not just to hear and read His Word, but to "keep those things which are written in it." And among the "things" written in it are the three angels' messages, which not only warn us about the trouble that's coming but show us the only hope we can have when it does. Compared to what's on TikTok or MTV, these are messages that we need to hear!

The first message begins with these words: "Then I saw another angel flying in the midst of heaven" (Revelation 14:6). What or who is this angel?

Both in Hebrew and in Greek, the word "angel" means a "messenger," someone with something to communicate with others. Though angels are supernatural beings from other parts of the cosmos, often coming with messages, information, to relay to God's people (see Daniel 9:20-23; Luke 1:11-38), the Bible at times applies the term to humans who come bearing messages as well.

Perhaps the most obvious case is John the Baptist. Talking about John in Matthew 11:9, 10, Jesus Himself, after giving a quick description of John and calling him not only a prophet but "more than a prophet," quoted the Old Testament (Malachi 3:1), saying:

"For this is he of whom it is written:

'Behold, I send My messenger before Your face,

Who will prepare Your way before You.' "

Jesus applies that text to John, even though the Hebrew word for "messenger" here is the same Hebrew word used all through the Old Testament for "angel," in reference to these supernatural beings who, in most of their appearances, bring messages from heaven to earth. In other words, both humans and angels are messengers from God.

In the case of the first angel, given the symbolic nature of the book of Revelation, and the context that follows—that of preaching to the world—the "angel" here is clearly referring to human messengers, with, however, a message from heaven. After all, throughout the Bible it is people whom God uses to witness to the world about Him. In the famous Great Commission, Jesus said: "Go therefore and make disciples of all the nations, baptizing them in the name of the Father and of the Son and of the Holy Spirit, teaching them to observe all things that I have commanded you; and lo, I am with you always, even to the end of the age" (Matthew 28:19, 20). He addressed these words to His people, His followers, His church. Historically it has been human beings who preach the gospel, which is what is happening with the three angels' messages, kind of the Great Commission contextualized for the last days.

Also, the text says that John saw "*another* angel," implying that other angels came before. Which makes sense. The book of Revelation covers the history of the church from Jesus' first coming to His second, and during all this time, however many angelic messengers might have made some appearances in Christian history (see Acts 12:7), the spread of the gospel around the world has been accomplished almost exclusively by human agents, human messenger—human *angels*.

What, then, does this human angel, these human messengers with a message from heaven, have to say that's so important, that can offer us hope in a world that, day by day, seems to offer us less and less?

The Thief on the Cross

One of the most famous accounts in Scripture is that of the thief on the cross, one of the two men crucified with Jesus by the Romans in A.D. 31. What happened?

Jesus of Nazareth, after a three-and-a-half-year ministry in the Holy Land, mostly Galilee in the north and Judea in the south, angered the religious establishment, who, fearing for its authority, wanted to have this Jesus killed. After talking about the danger posed by the Romans, the high priest for that year, Caiaphas, had said: "You know nothing at all, nor do you consider that it is expedient for us that one man should die for the people, and not that the whole nation should perish" (John 11:49, 50). That one man was Jesus, and "from that day on, they plotted to put Him to death" (verse 53). Their plotting succeeded, and they had Jesus crucified on a cross.

But Jesus wasn't alone there. "There were also two others, criminals, led with Him to be put to death. And when they had come to the place called Calvary, there they crucified Him, and the criminals, one on the right hand and the other on the left" (Luke 23:32, 33). The Gospel of Mark, recounting the same events, gave more information. "With Him they also crucified two robbers, one on His right and the other on His left. So the Scripture was fulfilled which says, 'And He was numbered with the transgressors'" (Mark 15:27, 28).

According to Mark, these men were robbers. However harsh Roman law could be, the two most likely were not crucified for stealing bread in order to feed a hungry family. Crucifixion was, generally, for the worst offenders, especially those who threatened Roman authority. Mark also portrays what happened with these men as a fulfillment of an Old Testament messianic prophecy, the famous Isaiah 53 chapter—a powerful depiction, more than a half century earlier, of Jesus' death. Mark quoted from verse 12 of that chapter, which, in talking about Jesus, said that "He was numbered with the transgressors." Mark saw the "transgressors" as the two robbers crucified with Jesus.

Though there are different terms in Hebrew for sins, sinners, transgression, iniquity, and so forth, the Hebrew noun used in verse 12 for "transgressors," *peshaim*, depicts the worst kind of sin and sinner. The root word often is translated as "rebellion" or "rebel." Isaiah, for instance, in another place wrote: "Hear, O heavens, and give ear, O earth! For the Lord has spoken: 'I have nourished and brought up children, and they have rebelled [same root as *peshaim*] against Me'" (Isaiah 1:2).

These men, then, these *peshaim*, were not innocent bystanders who, in the heat of the moment, found themselves crucified with Jesus. They were criminals deemed worthy not just of death but of the harshest kind of death, crucifixion. One of the two even admitted that "we receive the due reward of our deeds."

Luke continues to depict the events. "And the people stood looking on. But even the rulers with them sneered, saying, 'He saved others; let Him save Himself if He is the Christ, the chosen of God.' The soldiers also mocked Him, coming and offering Him sour wine, and saying, 'If You are the King of the Jews, save Yourself'" (Luke 23:35-37).

The crowd, other Jews, mocked Jesus as the Christ, the Messiah; the Roman soldiers, not interested in Jewish theology, mocked Him as a political figure, the King of the Jews.

Luke then focuses on the two criminals crucified with Jesus. "Then one of the criminals who were hanged blasphemed Him, saying, 'If You are the Christ, save Yourself and us.' But the other, answering, rebuked him, saying, 'Do you not even fear God, seeing you are under the same condemnation? And we indeed justly, for we receive the due reward of our deeds; but this Man has done nothing wrong'" (Luke 23:39-41).

Mark, in depicting the two thieves crucified with Christ, had them both attacking Jesus at first. "Even those who were crucified with Him reviled Him" (Mark 15:32). This second thief, however, watching what was happening—perhaps even hearing Jesus pray, "Father, forgive them, for they do not know what they do" (Luke 23:34)—had a change of heart, obviously. Somehow, amid the pain, the suffering, the turmoil, he was able to see Jesus as the crucified Savior. At that moment, besides Jesus, this dying criminal was the only human being in the world who knew who Jesus was and what was happening there, at the cross. This explains the thief's next words to Jesus: "Lord, remember me when You come into Your kingdom" (verse 42).

And what did Jesus say to this dying man, a criminal, a robber, one of the *peshaim*, someone who admitted his own guilt?

Well, friend, I'd like to help you, but you violated the eighth commandment, "Thou shalt not steal"? Or did He say, *Well, friend, I'd like to do something for you, but you were cursing Me when we first got here, right?* Or did Jesus say, *Well, friend, I'd like to do something for you, but people of your character and with your sinful past cannot come into My kingdom?*

Was that, or anything like that, what Jesus said?

Instead, looking at this man who had nothing to offer Him, a man whose only relationship to God's law seemed to be to violate it, a man who even by Roman standards was deemed worthy of death, Jesus, without any hesitation, waffling, or fine print, declared to him, "You will be with Me in paradise" (verse 43). In other words: *Well, friend, despite your cursing Me, despite your sinful past, despite your crimes, your sins, your thievery, and despite pretty much everything about you and your character—because of your faith in Me I am telling you, right now, that you have the promise of eternal life.*

How could this be? How could Jesus justly and fairly give such assurance to a man who had nothing to commend him to God, a man who by about any standard, even a worldly standard, had nothing righteous or holy about him? What did that man do to deserve what Jesus had so clearly and boldly offered him?

The answer is found in the first angel's message of Revelation 14. And it is captured with the phrase "the everlasting gospel."

The Good News

"Then I saw another angel flying in the midst of heaven, having the everlasting gospel to preach to those who dwell on the earth—to every nation, tribe, tongue, and people" (Revelation 14:6).

Most people have at least heard the word "gospel." When someone says "It's the gospel truth" about anything, even something secular, the idea is that it's a certain truth, a sure truth, something reliable. That concept fits perfectly with the "gospel" as it is revealed in the Bible. And particularly in the first angel's message, with its "everlasting" (NKJV) or "eternal" (NIV) gospel. It is the most certain, the most reliable, truth in all the creation.

But what does the Bible mean by the term "gospel"? One great example can be found in Matthew 11:5. John the Baptist, a prophet who helped announce the coming of Jesus, had been thrown into prison and wasn't, it seemed, getting out any time soon (in fact, he got out only as a headless corpse [see Matthew 14:10]). Discouraged by his imprisonment, he began to wonder about Jesus, to have doubts perhaps about Him, and when he had asked Jesus if He really were the "one who is to come" (Matthew 11:3, NIV), that is, the Messiah, Jesus responded like this: "Go and tell John what you hear and see: the blind receive their sight and the lame walk, lepers are cleansed and the deaf hear, and the dead are raised up, and the poor have good news preached to them" (verses 4, 5, ESV).

The "good news" preached to the poor is another way of expressing "the gospel." The New King James Version translates it: "And the poor have the gospel preached to them."

The "gospel" comes from a Greek word from which the English words "evangelism" or "evangelize" are derived. But the basic Greek meaning is to proclaim good and hopeful news about something. And in the case of the Bible, the gospel, the good and hopeful news, is the good and hopeful news about Jesus Christ and His coming to the earth.

Here are just a few of the almost 100 times the word is used in the New Testament. (A Hebrew parallel word, *bsr,* appears in the Old Testament, such as in Isaiah 61:1, a verse that Jesus Himself used in reference to His own mission of preaching the gospel [Luke 4:18].)

"And this gospel of the kingdom will be preached in all the world as a witness to all the nations, and then the end will come" (Matthew 24:14).

"Now it happened on one of those days, as He taught the people in the temple and preached the gospel, that the chief priests and the scribes, together with the elders, confronted Him" (Luke 20:1).

"For I am not ashamed of the gospel of Christ, for it is the power of God to salvation for everyone who believes, for the Jew first and also for the Greek" (Romans 1:16).

"In Him you also trusted, after you heard the word of truth, the gospel of your salvation; in whom also, having believed, you were sealed with the Holy Spirit of promise" (Ephesians 1:13).

In each of these verses, one could simply replace the word "gospel" with the words "good news," and the message would be the same. The gospel is the good news of what Jesus Christ has done for everyone, *everyone*, in the world.

Which is what? That is, if there ever were a time that everyone, as in *everyone*, needed some good news, it would be now, would it not? And so, what is the good news of the gospel, the "everlasting gospel," of the first angel's message?

The Gospel in Less Than 200 Words

A young man sat in a car, at night, next to a friend who, though an atheist, was struggling with that belief. At times this backsliding skeptic started to think that God, some God or another, had to exist. After all, nothing created itself. To create yourself, you would have to have already existed, and so anything that once didn't exist but came into existence had to have originated from something other than itself.

The car that they sat in, for instance, didn't come from itself, didn't create itself. The air that he breathed didn't come from itself; something prior to the air had to have created it. The solar system didn't create itself either. And even the universe, however it got started, didn't start itself. Something had to have made it—and who or what would that be but God?

And, too, the beauty, the complexity, of life, of nature. Though society and science and everyone insisted that the universe arose by chance, and that all the beauty and wonders of life were created without any intention or forethought at all—it just didn't seem right to him. To think that more conscious, planned, and intentional thought went into someone spray-painting graffiti on the side of a bridge than went into the creation of life, whether a bumblebee or the human brain, just seemed too much of a stretch. And all the wonderful fruit and vegetables, so tasty, so healthy, so beautiful, and so adapted to human needs—all with their own seeds in them? These, too, spoke to him of something more than pure chance, more than pure luck. They spoke to him of a conscious Creator.

And though His Christian friend explained to him about the great controversy, and the freedom inherent in love, and the risk inherent in freedom, still the question of evil bothered him. In short, this struggling atheist wondered what this God, if He existed (and he was more convinced that He did), was really like.

"Tell me," he said to his Christian friend, "in less than 200 words, what your God is like."

"OK," his friend said. "The God whom I worship created the entire universe. Every atom in every star in every one of the 2 trillion galaxies was not only created by this God but is sustained every moment by Him as well. This same God, the Creator, 2,000 years ago, 'shrank down,' and became a human infant in the womb of a Jewish peasant woman in the land of ancient Israel. That infant was born as the baby Jesus, and though human like us, He nevertheless lived a sinless life, a perfect life. And then this Jesus, God in the flesh, freely offered Himself as a sacrifice for sin, for the sin and evil of the whole human race. In other words, the punishment that each human being deserved for the evil that each human being has done, Jesus, God Himself, bore that punishment in Himself so that none of us have to face it ourselves. You want to know what God is like. Look at Jesus dying on the cross so that, in a sense, you don't have to. That is what God is like—in under 200 words."

Though knowing something about Christianity, the atheist never knew what his friend had just said. He was astonished, saying, "Wow! That sure is incredibly hopeful, isn't it? It sure gives you some encouragement about life."

"Yeah," the Christian said. "That's why they call it the 'good news.'"

The Sin Problem

No wonder the atheist was astonished. He should have been. God, the Creator, not only coming to this earth *but offering Himself as a sacrifice for the humans on it?* What was the situation here that was so dire, so bad, that it took this, the self-sacrifice of the Creator, to solve it?

In one sense it's not that hard to see how dire things are. Left to ourselves, we have no hope. Years ago a well-known atheist biologist, W. D. Hamilton, who loved to study Amazonian beetles, passed away. At the funeral in England his wife's eulogy went, in part, like this: "Bill, now your body is lying in the Wytham woods, but from here you will reach again your beloved forests. You will live not only in a beetle, but in billions of spores of fungi and algae. Brought by the wind higher up in the troposphere, all of you will form the clouds and, wandering across oceans, will fall down and fly up again and again, till eventually a drop of rain will join you to the water of the flooded forest of the Amazon."

Floating around in spores of fungi and algae? Not the most thrilling of prospects, or the most glorious ending to a human existence, is it? But what else does life, in and of itself, without something supernatural, without something divine, offer us?

"I stare," wrote Japanese author Haruki Murakami, "at this ceaseless, rushing crowd and imagine a time a hundred years from now. In a hundred years everybody here—me included—will have disappeared from the face of the earth and turned into ashes or dust. A weird thought, but everything in front of me starts to seem unreal, like a gust of wind could blow it all away."

Or, as the author of *The Book of Dead Philosophers* expressed it:

33

"This book begins from the simple assumption: what defines human life on our corner of the planet at the present time is not just a fear of death, but an overwhelming terror of annihilation. This is a terror both of the inevitability of our demise with its future prospect of pain and possibly meaningless suffering, and the horror of what lies in the grave other than our body nailed in a box and lowered into the earth to become worm food."

But that's just life, we're told. That's just the way it is, and we need to accept it. But according to the Bible, *that's not just the way it is.* It's not even close to the way it is. The whole purpose of Jesus Christ coming to the earth, of God in the flesh "shrinking down" and becoming one of us, to die for us—the whole purpose was to give every human being the opportunity for eternal life, the life that we had originally been created to have from the start.

The world has it all wrong. Radically wrong. Instead of death being the means of life—that is, through billions of years of violence, predation extinction, as evolution teaches—death was never meant to be here to begin with. We, as human beings, had been originally created to live forever. We were never created nor wired to die. It's the most unnatural of all human acts. Death was never supposed to be part of our equation, never. Death is not, as we are told, "part of life," but the opposite of life. It is the undoing of life. Death is an alien, an intruder who one day will be eradicated.

How, then, did death, this intruder, this "enemy" (1 Corinthians 15:26) that was never supposed to be here, get here? The apostle Paul makes it plain: "Therefore, just as through one man sin entered the world, and death through sin, and thus death spread to all men, because all sinned" (Romans 5:12).

That's it. Adam brought sin, sin leads to death, and because we all have been infected by sin and corrupted by sin, we all suffer the death that sin brings. After Adam and Eve (using the freedom inherent in love) sinned, everything changed, not only their own physical nature but nature itself (see Genesis 3:16-19), and death, suffering, corruption has been the lot of all humanity since. We're so used to these evils that we see them as the natural course of things, even though death, suffering, evil, and pain are no more "natural" than cancer.

Someone has said that the one Christian doctrine that you don't need to take on faith is the doctrine of human sinfulness. We see it all over. Look at the world: everything from war, to the growing gap between the rich and the poor, to human trafficking. Everywhere our sinfulness, our evil, is on display, as in a horror film.

Paul, writing 2,000 years ago, quoted Old Testament texts written maybe 1,000 years earlier than when he lived. And what did they say?

" 'There is none who understands;
There is none who seeks after God.
They have all turned aside;
They have together become unprofitable;
There is none who does good, no, not one.'
'Their throat is an open tomb;
With their tongues they have practiced deceit';
'The poison of asps is under their lips';
'Whose mouth is full of cursing and bitterness.'
'Their feet are swift to shed blood;
Destruction and misery are in their ways;
And the way of peace they have not known.'
'There is no fear of God before their eyes'" (Romans 3:11-18).

Three thousand years ago, 2,000 years ago, yesterday. It's all the same.

On December 17, 1903—after millennia of the human quest to fly—the Wright brothers got us off the ground in the first sustained flight of a powered, heavier-than-air aircraft. What a feat! By November 1, 1911, Lieutenant Giulio Gavotti, flying over a Turkish military camp in Libya, threw four small grenades, by hand, over the side of the plane in the world's first recorded aerial bombardment. What a feat, too! We learned how to fly, and about eight years later what do we do with our new wings but drop bombs on each other? If that isn't humanity, what is?

Charles Manson was the mastermind behind the murders of the actress Sharon Tate and others in California in the 1960s. Manson's mother had been a prostitute, and allegedly, one day when little Charlie was about 3, she was in a bar with him, and a barmaid looked over the bar and said, "What a cute kid. What can I give you for him?"

"How about," his mother answered, "a pitcher of beer?"

Any wonder little Charlie didn't grow up to be a model citizen? No, and the sins of the mother reverberated way beyond the bar, too. But that's the way it is with sin. And what do you get after 6,000 years of it? You get our present world.

But, someone says, *I'm not that bad.*

Probably not. But who would like to one day stand before God, a God who knows your every wrong thought, your every hidden deed, every single thing that you might have done in secret, things that you'd rather die than have revealed? How well, then, would you, covered in your own filthy garments, fare before a holy, sinless, perfect God? Sure, you might not be Charles Manson, or even his prostitute mother. But you're bad enough.

So bad, in fact, that it took the death of Jesus, of the Creator Himself, to solve the problem of sin. That is, only the self-sacrifice of the Creator—the one who made the heavens and the earth—*could atone for human evil.* If we could somehow work our way out of it, wouldn't that have been better than God crucified on the cross? The severity of the sin problem, of the death problem, of the evil problem, is best revealed by the severity of what it cost to solve it: Jesus crucified.

"Let this mind be in you which was also in Christ Jesus, who, being in the form of God, did not consider it robbery to be equal with God, but made Himself of no reputation, taking the form of a bondservant, and coming in the likeness of men.

And being found in appearance as a man, He humbled Himself and became obedient to the point of death, even the death of the cross" (Philippians 2:5-8).

The gospel, the sacrifice of Jesus, the Son of God—the one "through whom also He made the worlds; who being the brightness of His glory and the express image of His person, and upholding all things by the word of His power" (Hebrews 1:2, 3)—that is the solution. Only God, only someone greater than the creation, outside of the creation, transcendent to the creation—only His own self-sacrifice could atone for the creation. And that's what we have with Jesus. And what He did for us is known as the "everlasting gospel."

The Everlasting Gospel

The first angel's message begins with the "everlasting" gospel. Or the "eternal" gospel. The eternal good news. However often the word "gospel" itself appears in the Bible, this is the only time it was modified with the word "everlasting" (*aiōnios*), a term that John uses in other places with the word "life"; that is, in reference to the "eternal life" that we can have in Jesus. Such as: "Most assuredly, I say to you, he who believes in Me has everlasting life" (John 6:47).

The gospel is eternal because it was formulated by God in eternity, and it remained hidden until made manifest in Jesus. In fact, the gospel, the hope of eternal life for us all, had been formulated even *before* the world began. Look at these words, from Paul: "Blessed be the God and Father of our Lord Jesus Christ, who has blessed us with every spiritual blessing in the heavenly places in Christ, just as He chose us in Him before the foundation of the world, that we should be holy and without blame before Him in love" (Ephesians 1:3, 4).

Chosen in Him before the foundation of the world! Before we even existed, God's plan was for all of us to have salvation in Him. This isn't predestination, the idea that God chooses some to be saved, some to be lost. No, everyone, every human being, was predestined for salvation. God's plan, even before the world began, was for everyone to have eternal life in His Son.

"But we see Jesus, who was made a little lower than the angels for the suffering of death, crowned with glory and honour; that he by the grace of God should taste death for every man" (Hebrews 2:9, KJV). Why die for every "man" if it weren't planned for every man to be saved, even if every man in the end won't be?

"All we like sheep have gone astray; we have turned everyone to his own way; and the Lord hath laid on him the iniquity of us all" (Isaiah 53:6, KJV). Why take the iniquity "of us all" if the intention wasn't to pardon "us all"? People not availing themselves of the provision doesn't limit the provision any more than people starving themselves to death in a rich marketplace means there's not enough food.

It goes back to the idea, stressed earlier, that we had originally been created for eternal life. From the start we were to have lived forever. But even before God created this world, He knew what was going to happen; He knew that humanity would fall. And so, even before He had created us, He instituted the plan by which we all, every one of us, could be saved. That was the *everlasting* gospel.

"Paul, a servant of God and an apostle of Jesus Christ to further the faith of God's elect and their knowledge of the truth that leads to godliness—in the hope of eternal life, which God, who does not lie, promised before the beginning of time" (Titus 1:1, 2, NIV). Before the foundation of the world was one thing; Paul, though, pushes it back further: We were promised eternal life before the beginning of time. *Of time?* How interesting in light of modern science, which teaches that billions of years ago matter, energy, space, and time were created at once. Time itself had a beginning; it once did not exist. And, according to Paul, it was then—before its beginning, before time itself—that God promised us the hope of eternal life. Whenever exactly that was, who knows? We can be sure, though, that it was long ago. No wonder it's called the *everlasting* gospel.

"Forasmuch as ye know that ye were not redeemed with corruptible things, as silver and gold, from your vain conversation received by tradition from your fathers; but with the precious blood of Christ, as of a lamb without blemish and without spot: Who verily was foreordained before the foundation of the world, but was manifest in these last times for you" (1 Peter 1:18-20, KJV).

Before the foundation of the world the promise of salvation was given because, before the foundation of the world, the plan of salvation was too. Before time itself the Godhead planned that Jesus, the Son of God, would shed His blood for the human race. No wonder Jesus is called "the Lamb slain from the foundation of the world" (Revelation 13:8). The plan of salvation was laid out before we needed it, in order that it would be there when we did. It was the warranty on our souls.

And it has been the same gospel, the same plan of salvation, from before time began to the gospel being proclaimed in the first angel's message. There is only one gospel, and it first formulated in eternity past, and its fruits will last for eternity future. Paul himself stated, even warned, that "even if we, or an angel from heaven, preach any other gospel to you than what we have preached to you, let him be accursed.

As we have said before, so now I say again, if anyone preaches any other gospel to you than what you have received, let him be accursed" (Galatians 1:8, 9).

This gospel was first proclaimed to Adam and Eve in Eden (Genesis 3:15), after they fell and brought sin and death to our world. This same gospel was preached to Abraham. "And the Scripture, foreseeing that God would justify the Gentiles by faith, preached the gospel to Abraham beforehand, saying, 'In you all the nations shall be blessed'" (Galatians 3:8; see also Genesis 22:18). It was the same gospel preached to ancient Israel amid their wilderness wanderings (Hebrews 4:2). This same gospel, this same message, was what heaven had preached to shepherds outside Bethlehem about the birth of Jesus: "I bring you good tidings of great joy which will be to all people. For there is born to you this day in the city of David a Savior, who is Christ the Lord" (Luke 2:10, 11). It was the same gospel that Jesus preached: "The time is fulfilled, and the kingdom of God is at hand. Repent, and believe in the gospel" (Mark 1:15). It was the same gospel that saved the thief on the cross, to whom Jesus had promised eternal life (Luke 23:43). And it was the same gospel that Jesus told the disciples to preach until the very end: "And this gospel of the kingdom will be preached in all the world as a witness to all the nations, and then the end will come" (Matthew 24:14). And it is the same gospel, the "everlasting gospel," that the first angel proclaims to the world.

And the message, this eternal, everlasting message, is that salvation, the eternal life that we were originally supposed to have, is found only by faith in Jesus. Only by claiming, by faith, the perfect righteousness of Jesus, by leaning totally on His merits and not on ourselves or our good works, can we regain the eternal life that was supposed to have been ours from the start.

"Be not thou therefore ashamed of the testimony of our Lord, nor of me his prisoner: but be thou partaker of the afflictions of the gospel according to the power of God; who hath saved us, and called us with an holy calling, not according to our works, but according to his own purpose and grace, which was given us in Christ Jesus before the world began" (2 Timothy 1:8, 9, KJV).

If ever a text proved salvation by grace, and not by works, this must be it. If we were called to be saved before the world began, before time itself began, then salvation can't be based on our works, because we were called in Him before we even existed in order to have any works! Being promised something before you existed, before you could possibly have done anything to deserve it—if that is not grace, what is?

Also, as we have seen, Jesus, the one who created all that had been made (John 1:1-3), "shrinks down" and becomes a human baby who grew into adulthood, who lived a sinless life, who then offered that life as a sacrifice for us. *God Himself, dying for us?* As if that weren't enough to save us? We need our own works as well?

One Christian writer expressed it like this: "If you would gather together everything that is good and holy and noble and lovely in man and then present the subject to the angels of God as acting a part in the salvation of the human soul or in merit, the proposition would be rejected as treason. Standing in the presence of their Creator and looking upon the unsurpassed glory which enshrouds His person, they are looking upon the Lamb of God given from the foundation of the world to a life of humiliation, to be rejected of sinful men, to be despised, to be crucified. Who can measure the infinity of the sacrifice!" [1]

This, the "everlasting gospel," is the foundation of the three angels' messages, because without it, without the promise of eternal life, which is what the gospel is all about—what else matters? We'd be back to nothing more—*than what?* Than floating around as spores in the atmosphere or being lowered into a hole and becoming nothing but ashes and dust? Surely, after all we go through, all the toils and troubles and hassles of just getting by in life, to end like that, and forever, too, hardly seems worth it. Hardly makes sense at all.

It doesn't make sense, because it was never the way that it was supposed to have been. Sin derailed everything; the gospel, the "everlasting gospel," is God's way of restoring normalcy, sanity, and life to a world suffused in the abnormality and insanity of death.

From Heaven to Earth

"Then I saw another angel flying in the midst of heaven, having the everlasting gospel to preach to those who dwell on the earth—

---

[1] Ellen G. White, *Faith and Works* (Nashville: Southern Pub. Assn., 1979), p. 24.

to every nation, tribe, tongue, and people—saying with a loud voice, 'Fear God and give glory to Him, for the hour of His judgment has come; and worship Him who made heaven and earth, the sea and springs of water'" (Revelation 14:6, 7).

Notice the heaven-to-earth dynamic here: the first angel's message, though being physically delivered by humans, comes from heaven. It's of divine, not human, origin. It is revealed truth, truth that is told to us, truth divulged to us, truth given to us by God through His human messengers. These messengers, such as Moses, Isaiah, Jeremiah, Matthew, John, Paul, and Peter, had writings in the Bible; or they didn't, such as Nathan the prophet (2 Samuel 7:1, 2) or John the Baptist, of whom Jesus said that "among those born of women there is not a greater prophet than John the Baptist" (Luke 7:28). Either way, they were speaking for God.

Meanwhile, Scripture itself is "given by inspiration of God, and is profitable for doctrine, for reproof, for correction, for instruction in righteousness" (2 Timothy 3:16). The Greek word for "inspiration of God" is *theopneustos*, which means "God-breathed." It has been revealed by God Himself, "who cannot lie" (Titus 1:2). Humans lie, but not God, and so we must listen to what He has said to us in this angel's message.

Because this message comes from heaven, that is, from high above the earth, it is proclaimed to "those who dwell on the earth." The prophet Isaiah talks about high mountains (Isaiah 40:9; 52:7) as the place from which the gospel is preached to those below. Before sending His disciples to preach, Jesus said that what He had told them in secret would be proclaimed from rooftops (Matthew 10:27), high places from which their voices would be heard by the masses in the streets beneath.

The angel also speaks in a "loud voice," giving the idea of being easily heard. In biblical times, long before anything even like a telegraph wire transmitting Morse Code—much less FaceTime—ever entered anyone's imagination, messengers were trained from youth to have strong voices. These trained men, standing from posts on strategic mountains, would loudly shout to those on another mountain, and so forth, until the message reached the intended destination.

In short, this first angel's message will be proclaimed worldwide; no one will be able to claim ignorance. (This book you're reading right now is part of that prophetic truth being fulfilled.) The universality of this message is also found in whom it is being directed to: "to those who dwell on the earth—to every nation, tribe, tongue, and people." The phrase "who dwell on the earth" is also used in Revelation to depict people who have chosen not to follow and obey God (see Revelation 13:8, 14). However, because the first angel's message is a call to faithfulness, this phrase in this context must be referring to a time when people still have the opportunity to choose whom they will worship and obey (see "A Bit of Context, Please [Part Two]"). In fact, what follows right after, "every nation, tribe, tongue, and people," shows the universality of the message. It is for every human being.

Which makes sense. Humanity has been created, out the gate, to live forever; in order to ensure us of that eternal life (if we would accept it), God put in place "the everlasting gospel" long before anyone of us took our first, or last, breath. "For to this end we both labor and suffer reproach, because we trust in the living God, who is the Savior of all men, especially of those who believe" (1 Timothy 4:10). Thousands of years ago the Lord told Abram (later Abraham) that in him "all the families of the earth will be blessed" (Genesis 12:3). The destroying fires of hell were originally prepared only for the devil and his angels, not for humans and their offspring (Matthew 25:41).

The plan of salvation is, ultimately, a restoration: re-creating what has been ruined by sin and death. It's no wonder, then, that the first angel's message, proclaiming "the everlasting gospel," is for all humanity. Christ died for all people, with no one left out. The tragedy of the lost is that no one should be lost, not when such a steep price, the crucifixion of the Creator, has been paid for them to be saved.

Finally, in a world racked by ethnic, racial, and gender conflicts (when has it not, actually?), the universality of the gospel message should say something about the essential equality of humanity: we're all wretches, all in need of God's grace (go back to the idea, in "The Sin Problem," of you standing before a holy God who knows your deepest, ugliest secrets). Death cares nothing about race, gender, social standing, or wealth. It's an equal-opportunity destroyer. "Every nation, tribe, tongue, and people" are ultimately, and equally, impotent before it, because, sooner or later, death pulls "every nation, tribe, tongue and people" back into the dust and dirt from which they all arose. And that is why the first angel's message is directed to all of them, to all of us.

Mi-Yittan

Most languages come sprinkled with idioms, such as (in English) "not know jack," or "a lame duck," or "to be on cloud nine," whose meanings are not literally, or even logically, deduced from the phrases themselves. (To "not know jack" has nothing to do with a man named Jack, but refers to having no knowledge at all of a specific situation.)

Biblical Hebrew itself has idioms; one is *mi-yittan*, which literally means "Who will give?" However, it's used idiomatically to express something else. After their escape from Egypt, the children of Israel, facing challenges in the wilderness, exclaimed, "If only we had died by the Lord's hand in Egypt!" (Exodus 16:3, NIV). The phrase "if only" came from *mi-yittan*. In Psalm 14:7 David utters, "Oh that the salvation of Israel were come out of Zion!" (KJV). The Hebrew doesn't say, "Oh"; it says, *mi-yittan*, "Who will give?" In Job 6:8, when Job exclaims, "Oh, that I might have my request," "Oh" is translated, rather poorly, from *mi-yittan*.

In all these cases, *mi-yittan* expresses the idea of frailty and weakness in the face of events that the people cannot control as they would wish. Overcome by the sufferings that had so quickly choked but not strangled him, Job wished, "Oh, that I might have my request"—which is that God would have "cut me off" (Job 6:9, KJV); that is, let him die and be free from his trials. But God didn't, and his cry *mi-yittan*, "Who will give?" expresses the unfulfilled wish that God would.

Another occurrence appears in Deuteronomy 5:29. Going over the history of God's providences, Moses reminds the children of Israel about their request that he, Moses, talk to the Lord for them lest they die. According to Moses, the Lord, pleased with their request, then said: "Oh that there were such a heart in them, that they would fear me, and keep all my commandments always" (KJV). The word translated "Oh"? *Mi-yittan*.

Mi-yittan? Here is the Lord—the Creator God, the one who made space, time, and matter and energy, the one who spoke our world into existence, the one who breathed into Adam the breath of life—here is the Sovereign God Himself uttering a phrase associated with the weaknesses and limitations of humanity? Talk about the reality of free will. Talk about the limits of what God can do in the midst of the great controversy. This use of *mi-yittan* reveals that even God can't trample on free will (for the moment He did, it would no longer be free).

What's fascinating, too, is the context. The Lord wishes, *mi-yittan*, that His people would have such a heart as to fear Him. *To fear God?* Can't God easily make people fear Him, as in being scared of Him? At Mount Sinai, for instance, with the giving of the Ten Commandments, what happened? "When the people heard the thunder and the loud blast of the ram's horn, and when they saw the flashes of lightning and the smoke billowing from the mountain, they stood at a distance, trembling with fear. And they said to Moses, 'You speak to us, and we will listen. But don't let God speak directly to us, or we will die!'" (Exodus 20:19, NLT). Trembling in fear before God? The God who can open up and swallow people alive (Numbers 16:32) or bring fire down from heaven that burns up not just animal sacrifices but also "the wood and the stones and the dust" (1 Kings 18:38)? "And it licked up the water that was in the trench" (verse 38). This is a God who, if He chose to, could scare the daylights out of any of us (to use an English idiom). God cannot force people to love Him without destroying what love is, but God could easily force people to fear Him without destroying what fear is. If not free, we could not love God, but, free or not free, we could certainly cower in dreadful terror before Him.

Yet that's not the kind of fear that God wants from us. Look at the following texts, all about fearing God; look, too, at the positive, uplifting implications that come from fearing God. "Afterward the children of Israel shall return and seek the Lord their God and David their king. They shall fear the Lord and His goodness in the latter days" (Hosea 3:5). "The fear of the Lord is the beginning of knowledge" (Proverbs 1:7). "The eye of the Lord is on those who fear Him" (Psalm 33:18). "There is no want to those who fear Him" (Psalm 34:9). "He will bless those who fear the Lord" (Psalm 115:13). "He fulfills the desires of those who fear Him" (Psalm 145:19, NIV). "Therefore, having these promises, beloved, let us cleanse ourselves from all filthiness of the flesh and spirit, perfecting holiness in the fear of God" (2 Corinthians 7:1). "Honor all people. Love the brotherhood. Fear God. Honor the king" (1 Peter 2:17).

And then, too, there's the first angel. After we're told that this angel is proclaiming the everlasting gospel to all the world, the angel begins that proclamation with a loud voice, declaring, "Fear God and give glory to Him, for the hour of His judgment has come; and worship Him who made heaven and earth, the sea and springs of water" (Revelation 14:7). The first words out of his mouth are to "fear God." If that does not mean to be scared of Him, as you might be scared of a machine gun-toting, deranged psychotic rampaging through your neighborhood, what does it mean? And why would the first words spoken by an angel proclaiming the great news of Christ's death for us, the everlasting gospel—why would those first words be to "fear God"?

Section Three

Fear God

Why wouldn't the first words of an angel proclaiming the everlasting gospel be "Fear God"? Think, again, about what the everlasting gospel is. The God who created and sustains the universe, the estimated 50 billion-light-year-wide *observable* universe (who knows how far beyond even that it goes?), and whose power is so vast that our imaginations can't grasp His creation (how do you imagine something 50 billion light-years wide?)—this God so humbled Himself, so lowered Himself, that He purposely, of His own choice and out of love for us, allowed Himself to become one of us. "Let this mind be in you which was also in Christ Jesus, who, being in the form of God, did not consider it robbery to be equal with God, but made Himself of no reputation, taking the form of a bondservant, and coming in the likeness of men. And being found in appearance as a man, He humbled Himself and became obedient to the point of death, even the death of the cross" (Philippians 2:5-8).

It would have been an infinite condescension just to have stepped down from the glories of heaven to come to this fallen, disease- and war- and crime-ridden planet as a human being. After all, what is the earth in contrast to the vastness of the universe, with its estimated 2 trillion galaxies, each with billions of stars (and only God knows how many exoplanets[1] around those stars)? In the geography of the cosmos, our whole solar system, sun included, would seem of no more consequence or importance than a grain of sand digested in the belly of a crab. That's our solar system. What about our planet, earth, or each of us, which in contrast even to the earth are but fleeting spasms of cellular metabolism that will eventually all but evaporate into nothing but scanty chemical remains?

---

[1] Exoplanets are planets that orbit other stars.

And yet so great was His love for us that not only did He come to live among us but He—the Creator of the 50 billion-light-year-wide *observable* universe (who knows how far beyond even that it goes?)—allowed Himself to be mocked, jeered, humiliated, tortured, and then crucified for us so that we can all have the promise of eternal life.

No wonder we should fear Him, not as in being scared but as in being awed and utterly reverent and utterly astonished that He would care so much for us, even at such a cost to Himself. He is so powerful; we are so weak, we are so filthy, we are so sinful before Him that He could have justifiably wiped us out. But instead He humbled Himself and, reaching across the cold, dead inhospitable void of space, became one of us. And by His willful self-sacrifice, Jesus linked us to Himself with ties that will never be broken.

Fear God? Fear that in the face of such love, such undeserved love and such unrelenting grace, that we should sin against Him. Fear that we should have to stand before Him without His robe of righteousness. Fear that we should allow ourselves to forget His great love to us and reject His offer of salvation. That's a frightening thought: that despite the cross, that despite the astonishing self-abnegation of God Himself, that despite the infinite price paid for our souls, we should ignore or forget or reject what has already been done for us. Again, "before time began" (2 Timothy 1:9; Titus 1:2) each of us had been chosen in Him to have the eternal life that was supposed to have been ours from the start. And to secure this life for us, even before we existed, Christ covenanted with the Father and the Holy Spirit to sacrifice Himself for us as the only means of any of us having eternal life.

And yet, as too many will do—*to reject the offer?* To walk away from such infinite price paid for us? To count it as a small thing or to brush it aside for the fleeting pleasures of this world, which never gives true happiness and is passing away anyway?

That *is* a frightening thought!

Human analogies fail, but imagine someone drinks himself silly over long years until his liver is completely shot. A loved one, seeing what is happening, offers their own liver, at the cost of their life. The liver is removed, but the sick person then chooses not to take it, even after the person died so that they could have it. That, roughly, is what it means to reject, in the face of Calvary, what Christ has done for us.

In the past, people have looked up into the night sky filled with stars and felt a sense of awe, of fear, at the vastness, the grandeur, the beauty of what was up there above them while they were so small, so little, so seemingly insignificant below all this. And today telescopes that reveal a cosmos so vast that we throw out such numbers as 20 billion light-years[2] for these distances give us the illusion that we can grasp them when we can only shudder, in awe, in fear, at the infinitely starry magnificence that surrounds us. But if humans can be in awe of the creation itself, how much more so should we before the God who created it and who sustains it? That thought alone should be more than enough to get us to tremble before Him. But then, added to this, to realize our own unworthiness before Him and yet to know that despite this unworthiness—no, indeed, because of it—Christ sacrificed Himself for us?

Before such big ideas, before such cosmic love focused directly on us, how can we not cry out, *Who is sufficient for these things?* And also, how could we not ask: How are we supposed to respond? What response is worthy of what's been given us? And how could anything that we do be of consequence in contrast to what's been done for us in Jesus? The answer—and the first thing we're told to do, after to fear God—is to "give glory to Him" (Revelation 14:7).

Think of the Amoeba

In light of the astonishing truth that "so great was His [Christ's] love for us that not only did He come to live among us but He—the Creator of the 50 billion-light-year-wide *observable* universe (who knows how far beyond even that it goes?)—allowed Himself to be mocked, jeered, humiliated, tortured, and then crucified for us so that we can all have the promise of eternal life," it seems rather strange that we should be called to "give glory to Him."

Give glory to God? How could that possibly be? How can we, sinful, fallen beings on a tiny planet in a single galaxy out of 2 trillion galaxies, give glory to God? Considering how piddling we are in contrast, not

---

[2] That is, traveling at the speed of light, 186,000 miles per second (seven times around the earth in one second), a person would take 20 billion years to reach that far away.

only to the universe but to the God who created it; considering how sinful and fallen we are in contrast to a holy God; and considering how dependent we are upon God for salvation—the idea of us glorifying Him seems preposterous. It would be like a single-celled amoeba singing praises to us and we, actually, caring that it does.

Yet the theme of humans bringing glory to God pervades the Bible. Jesus Himself said, "Let your light so shine before men, that they may see your good works and glorify your Father in heaven" (Matthew 5:16). "I give thanks to you, O Lord my God, with my whole heart, and I will glorify your name forever" (Psalm 86:12, ESV). "So, whether you eat or drink, or whatever you do, do all to the glory of God" (1 Corinthians 10:31, ESV). "For you were bought with a price. So glorify God in your body" (1 Corinthians 6:20, ESV). "Let them give glory to the Lord and declare His praise in the coastlands" (Isaiah 42:12). "There is no one like You among the gods, O Lord, nor are there any works like Yours. All nations whom You have made shall come and worship before You, O Lord, and they shall glorify Your name" (Psalm 86:8-10, NASB). "My Father is glorified by this, that you bear much fruit, and so prove to be My disciples" (John 15:8, NASB).

This idea, that of fallen sinful humanity being able to glorify God and to give God glory, however initially counterintuitive (think of that amoeba), is biblical. What does it mean, especially in the context of the three angels' messages? Why, after being told about "the everlasting gospel," and being told to "fear God," are we told to "give glory to Him" as well? How do we do that—and why?

One of the most exciting moments in intellectual history came in 1687 when Sir Isaac Newton published a massive work called, in English, *Mathematical Principles of Natural Philosophy*. Though the story about Newton sitting under an apple tree and an apple falling on his head and he, suddenly, discovering gravity, is silly (everyone knew about gravity), what Newton did realize, and what he published in his book, was that this gravity (whatever it was?) pervaded the universe. The same force that caused an apple to fall to the ground was the same force that kept the moon and the planets in orbit. In fact, everything in the universe attracts each other with the force of gravity. Your reading this book exerts a gravitational pull on the moon, on the sun, and on the Crab Nebula. Though, yes, the attraction is weak, and the farther away things are, the weaker it gets, yet it's still real. In some strange way, everything in the universe is intertwined.

Something similar applies in the spiritual realm. Heaven and earth are more closely bound than we realize. What happens on earth impacts heaven, and what happens in heaven impacts earth. "For this reason I bow my knees to the Father of our Lord Jesus Christ," wrote the apostle Paul, "from whom the whole family in heaven and earth is named" (Ephesians 3:14, 15). *The whole family in heaven and earth?* Though exactly what Paul meant by the "whole family in heaven and earth" is debated, he certainly, by the word "family," gives the idea of some kind of closeness between heaven and earth.

Just a few verses before, Paul wrote that "God's purpose in all this was to use the church to display his wisdom in its rich variety to all the unseen rulers and authorities in the heavenly places" (Ephesians 3:10, NLT). The idea in this text (and as seen in the ones above about glorifying God) is similar: that our actions here matter, and that we can, indeed, bring glory to God. We can bring glory to God before men (Matthew 5:16), and, it seems, before "unseen rulers and authorities in the heavenly places" as well. Again, the universe is more tightly linked, at least spiritually, than what appears to our immediate senses.

One of the earliest books of the Bible, the book of Job, presents a powerful example of the close link between heaven and earth, and shows that what we do here matters, even greatly, to God. Though the story begins on earth, with a man named Job, it quickly shifts to some cosmic realm (heaven, perhaps), where Satan and other angels (sometimes referred to as the "sons of God"), are meeting. God Himself points to the person of Job, saying, "Have you considered My servant Job, that there is none like him on the earth, a blameless and upright man, one who fears God and shuns evil?" (Job 1:8). Satan then responds, basically saying, *Sure, God, no wonder he serves You. Look at how good his life is. Let Job's life go bad and see what happens. See if he really loves You after all!* (see Job 1:9-2:7). God then allows Satan to destroy Job's property, family, and health, and yet, amid it all, Job stayed faithful to God, proving Satan wrong. God used Job to refute the charges of Satan. That is, the actions of a human being here on earth had repercussions in heaven. That's how tightly linked heaven and earth are.

Though for thousands of years Bible students have pondered the meaning of this book, the point for now—as astonishing as it is (again, think of the amoeba)—is that God, the Creator, was in a sense "glorified" by Job's actions. Job proved that his love for God and his trust in God's goodness was so strong that despite all that happened, Job remained faithful. This is a powerful example of the principle behind Jesus' words: "My Father is glorified by this, that you bear much fruit, and so prove to be My disciples" (John 15:8, NASB). Also, the story of Job unfolded in the context of the great controversy between God and Satan. The battle is real, and our actions in it matter both in heaven and on earth.

In short, we as human beings, by staying faithful to God, by bearing much fruit, by "letting our lights shine," glorify God, as we have been told to do in the first angel's message.

Give Glory to God

However common the idea of God being glorified in and by His people, the actual phrase, to "give glory" to God, is not common in the Bible. But its use is instructive.

A powerful example came from early Israelite history, when the children of Israel, after wandering for 40 years in the desert, had finally crossed over into the Promised Land, which was filled with dangerous and corrupt pagans who, among other things, would sacrifice their own children to their "gods," such as Molech. Before the Hebrews had entered the land, they had been specifically warned against this horrific practice. "And you shall not let any of your descendants pass through the fire to Molech, nor shall you profane the name of your God: I am the Lord" (Leviticus 18:21). These Canaanites were bad folk who, it seemed, had long spurned God's overtures to them (Genesis 15:16). Notice, too, the idea: by doing this evil practice they would "profane" the name of their God; this is the opposite of the idea that, when doing well, when obeying the Lord, when letting their "lights shine," they would glorify that name instead.

The children of Israel had also been warned against the personal pillaging of these pagan nations. "And you, by all means abstain from the accursed things, lest you become accursed when you take of the accursed things, and make the camp of Israel a curse, and trouble it. But all the silver and gold, and vessels of bronze and iron, are consecrated to the Lord; they shall come into the treasury of the Lord" (Joshua 6:18, 19). These "accursed things," *herem* (in Hebrew), carries the idea of the utter destruction of something in order to protect the people from spiritual contagion. Israel's security in the land—as the chosen people, who had been called out to reveal the true God to a world suffused in idolatry, polytheism, and evil practices—depended upon their spiritual purity, and nothing endangered that purity more than being contaminated by their neighbors' evil. A good portion of the Old Testament reveals how much the Hebrew people allowed themselves, unfortunately, to be overcome by the very things that God had warned them against.

Early on, in fact, just after they had entered the Promised land, calamity struck, and the Lord told Joshua why: "Get up! Why do you lie thus on your face? Israel has sinned, and they have also transgressed My covenant which I commanded them. For they have even taken some of the accursed things, and have both stolen and deceived; and they have also put it among their own stuff" (Joshua 7:10, 11). The idea of mixing pagan things with their own symbolized what ultimately would lead to the nation's demise (a practice that, as we will see, has also plagued Christianity), and not long after they had entered the land, this contamination was already happening.

Out of greed, out of covetousness, and in flagrant disobedience to the commands of God, who did not want His people contaminated by *herem*, someone in the camp had pillaged for himself things from the recently destroyed pagan city of Jericho. Though having a chance to come clean and confess, only when he was confronted by the leader of the people at that time, Joshua (whom God showed who was guilty), did Achan admit his evil deed, saying: "Indeed I have sinned against the Lord God of Israel, and this is what I have done: When I saw among the spoils a beautiful Babylonian garment, two hundred shekels of silver, and a wedge of gold weighing fifty shekels, I coveted them and took them. And there they are, hidden in the earth in the midst of my tent, with the silver under it" (verses 20, 21).

When the situation was investigated and found true, Achan was immediately punished with death. "Why hast thou troubled us?" said Joshua. "The Lord shall trouble thee this day" (verse 25, KJV). Achan's sin had been committed in open defiance of direct and solemn warnings, all accompanied by manifestations of God's power—such as when, at the shouts of the people and the blowing of the trumpets, "the wall of Jericho fell down flat. Then the people went up into the city, every man straight before him, and they took the city" (Joshua 6:20). The fact that God's power alone had given the victory to Israel, that they had not taken Jericho by their own strength, gave solemn weight to the divine prohibition of taking the spoils for themselves.

However, when Joshua first confronted Achan, he said, "My son, I beg you, give glory to the Lord God of Israel, and make confession to Him, and tell me now what you have done; do not hide it from me"(Joshua 7:19). *Give glory to God*, just like the phrase in Revelation 14:7. In the context of judgment, of being called to admit his guilt, Achan is told to give glory to God. What does that mean? It's not to give glory as singing praises to Him. Instead, it's to admit that God is just in not only pointing out Achan's overt act of greed and selfishness and defiance, but also in the penalty that will come. Achan deserved the punishment that he is about to face, and he is expected to recognize this fact. In short, to give glory to God is to admit, in the context of judgment, that God's judgment is just and fair.

Considering the great controversy, and God's intention to deal with sin and rebellion and evil in a manner harmonious with the principles of love, and not force—how important not only that God's judgment be just but that others, including "the principalities and powers in heavenly places" (Ephesians 3:10), acknowledge that justice. In fact, Revelation 19:1, 2 depicts some of these "principalities and powers" in heavenly places shouting: "Alleluia! Salvation and glory and honor and power belong to the Lord our God! For true and righteous are His judgments."

Which is why this specific phrase, to "give glory" to God, appears in other settings of divine judgment as well (1 Samuel 6:5; Jeremiah 13:15, 16; Malachi 2:2). But, no question, the most dramatic, consequential, and powerful example occurs in the heart of the first angel's message itself: "Fear God and give glory to Him, for the hour of His judgment has come." Why "fear God"? Why "give glory to Him"? Because the hour, the time, of His judgment, God's judgment, has come.

Judgment? God's judgment? An all-knowing, all-seeing God who knows your every thought, your every secret deed, your everything including the things that you have long ago forgotten? That judgment?

What are your odds?

Stop Worrying?

Years ago British atheists started a campaign in which those famous red double-decker London buses carried this sign: "THERE'S PROBABLY NO GOD. NOW STOP WORRYING AND ENJOY YOUR LIFE."

Probably no God? (Hedging their bets, huh?)

Why, though, worry if there were a God? Because perhaps this God has a moral standard, such as the Ten Commandments, which people would be obligated to follow, as opposed to their own personal standards that often rise no higher than their own urges and lusts? Stop worrying about having to answer to this God for the evil things that they have done to others, or even to children, and that they have gotten away with, at least so far. The mere idea of this God implies a sense of moral obligation, of moral accountability—precisely what those behind the bus campaign obviously worried about. And rightly so, considering that the Bible itself depicts human depravity—"that every mouth may be stopped, and all the world may become guilty before God" (Romans 3:19)—in stark terms (see "The Sin Problem"). The phraseology of this sign, with its appeal to "stop worrying," reveals their fear of a moral God whose existence they try to deny.

A young man who was an agnostic was, by the cultural and social customs of his day, not so bad. Yet every now and then he would think: *Maybe there really is some God out there?* But each time that thought came, he'd push it out of his mind. Why? Because if there were a God out there, he knew he was in deep trouble! Those who put up the London bus signs had, obviously, similar fears.

55

And again, with good reason, too. To quote from "The Sin Problem": "But who would like to one day stand before God, a God who knows your every wrong thought, your every hidden deed, every single thing that you might have done in secret, things that you'd rather die than have revealed? How well, then, would you, covered in your own filthy garments, fare before a holy, sinless, perfect God? Sure, you might not be Charles Manson, or even his prostitute mother. But you're bad enough."

Even worse: if these atheists are right about there being no God, then think about what that would also mean as far as justice ever being done in a world that, since the dawn of recorded history, has cried out for justice. If "there's probably no God," then there's probably no hope of justice, no hope of answers, no hope of untold wrongs being righted, of untold evil being accounted for and punished. Every unpunished and unaccounted evil will forever remain unpunished and unaccounted for—a depressing and hopeless thought.

Ever heard of the Pinto? It was the brainchild of the Ford Motor Company in the 1970s, an attempt to compete with the Volkswagen Beetle. Yet the company, including its iconic executive, Lee Iacocca, knew that the Pinto was unsafe, and that if their car were rear-ended, even at a relatively slow speed, the gas tank would explode. However, doing a cost-benefit analysis, Ford decided to sell the car anyway, dangerous flaws and all, figuring that it would be cheaper to pay the lawsuits for the deaths and maiming than it would be to make the car right.

"What caught the public's eye in the Pinto cases was the disclosure that Ford found it cheaper to pay off the families of the victims of Pinto fires than the $137 million it would cost to fix the Pinto immediately, according to an internal Ford memo introduced during a civil trial. That meant it was not cost-effective to do the repairs."[3]

Hundreds of passengers were killed, scorched, maimed, including a 13-year-old boy who was burned over 90 percent of his body, because Lee Iacocca and others at Ford decided on profit over people. Pintos blowing up and burning passengers, however, wasn't good PR for Ford, whose radio advertising spots included the line "Pinto leaves you with that warm feeling." The spots, along with the Pinto, were

---

[3] https://www.autonews.com/article/20030616/SUB/306160770/lee-iacocca-s-pinto-a-fiery-failure

eventually pulled, but not until after the unsafe vehicle had left a trail of carnage and death.

Yet Lee Iacocca went on to fame and immense fortune and died at the ripe old age of 94, a revered figure in American business.

Justice?

If "there's probably no God," then, as poet Czeslaw Milosz warned, there is "nothingness after death—the huge solace of thinking that for our betrayals, greed, cowardice, murders we are not going to be judged."[4] Of course, for some, that's exactly what they want: no judgment for their betrayals, greed, cowardice, and all the other evils humans have been guilty of but have never had to answer for.

Only one problem: if the Bible teaches anything, *anything*, it teaches, again and again—Old Testament, New Testament, from Moses to Paul, from parables, to poetry, to flat-out in-your-face warnings—that God is a God of justice and a God of judgment, and that human beings will be made to answer for all their deeds here, all the deeds and evil that they think that they have gotten away with.

Just a smattering of the Bible promises that awaits the evil so far unpunished:

"Look, I am coming soon, bringing my reward with me to repay all people according to their deeds" (Revelation 22:12, NLT).

"God will judge us for everything we do, including every secret thing, whether good or bad" (Ecclesiastes 12:14, NLT).

"But the Lord reigns forever,

executing judgment from his throne.

He will judge the world with justice

and rule the nations with fairness" (Psalm 9:7, 8, NLT).

"And do you think this, O man, you who judge those practicing such things, and doing the same, that you will escape the judgment of God?" (Romans 2:3).

"But the heavens and the earth which are now preserved by the same word, are reserved for fire until the day of judgment and perdition of ungodly men" (2 Peter 3:7).

"Fear God and give glory to Him, for the hour of His judgment has come; and worship Him who made heaven and earth, the sea and

---

[4] Czeslaw Milosz, *Road-Side Dog* (New York: Farrar, Strauss, Giroux, 1998), p. 22.

springs of water" (Revelation 14:7).

For the hour of His judgment *has come*. What does that mean? And also, what hope can we, as sinners, as people who also have done things that have gone unpunished—what hope can we have in this judgment as well?

Section Four

The Hour of His Judgment

"For it is time for judgment to begin at the household of God; and if it begins with us, what will be the outcome for those who do not obey the gospel of God?" (1 Peter 4:17, ESV).

"I tell you, on the day of judgment people will give account for every careless word they speak, for by your words you will be justified, and by your words you will be condemned" (Matthew 12:36, 37, ESV).

"Because he has fixed a day on which he will judge the world in righteousness by a man whom he has appointed; and of this he has given assurance to all by raising him from the dead" (Acts 17:31, ESV).

We could go on and on: Bible text after Bible text about God as a God of judgment, and the certainty from heaven above that the injustice and evil on earth below will, one day, be accounted for, answered, and justly punished. The concept of God's judgments permeates the Scriptures. There's not one single overarching judgment that rights all wrongs, that punishes all evil, and that rewards all goodness. Instead, God's judgments have been ongoing events depending upon the time and place and circumstances, and from His judgments in the past we can learn about the judgment now and to come.

From God bringing judgment to Adam and Eve after the Fall (Genesis 3:14-19), to the worldwide flood (Genesis 7), to the destruction of Sodom and Gomorrah (Genesis 19), to the fall of ancient Babylon (Daniel 5), to the declaration of judgment in the first angel's message today, to the final judgment at the very end of time (Revelation 20)—the Bible reveals the reality of God's judgments.

Such as one powerful and particularly relevant depiction of judgment found in the Old Testament book of Daniel. In chapter 7 the prophet had a prophetic dream of four beasts arising out of the sea (verse 3), each one symbolic of a world empire (verse 17) that would arise and then vanish into ancient history until a massive judgment in heaven (verses 9, 10, 22, 26) leads to God's eternal kingdom (verses 14, 22, 27). The main point of prophetic dream is to show that these four earthly and transient kingdoms are followed, ultimately, by God's eternal one: "Those great beasts, which are four, are four kings which arise out of the earth. But the saints of the Most High shall receive the kingdom, and possess the kingdom forever, even forever and ever" (verses 17, 18).

These four earthly kingdoms, or empires, have long been identified as Babylon, Media-Persia, Greece, and then Rome, the final empire, which remains until the end of this present world. Rome, the Rome of the republic and then the Caesars, was the phase of Rome that arose right after ancient Greece. However, Rome, this fourth power, still exists today (just as the prophecy predicted, because it remains until the end of the world), but now in the papal phase. In fact, the fourth beast had been described with certain characteristics that fit medieval Rome very well, which included, unfortunately, great persecution (verses 21, 24, 25).

Different times in this chapter (verses 9, 10, 22, 26) an end-time heavenly judgment is depicted as leading to God's eternal kingdom, what the Bible calls "a new heaven and a new earth" (Revelation 21:1; see also Isaiah 65:17; 66:22; 2 Peter 3:13).

The first goes like this: "I beheld till the thrones were cast down, and the Ancient of days did sit, whose garment was white as snow, and the hair of his head like the pure wool: his throne was like the fiery flame, and his wheels as burning fire. A fiery stream issued and came forth from before him: thousand thousands ministered unto him, and ten thousand times ten thousand stood before him: the judgment was set, and the books were opened" (Daniel 7:9, 10, KJV).

The "Ancient of Days" (a name for God), thrones, books open, judgment set. Clearly some kind of cosmic courtroom scene is unfolding before all these other heavenly beings, which—given what we have seen about the great controversy and the interest of "the principalities and powers in the heavenly places" (Ephesians 3:10)—should not be surprising.

This same judgment is later shown like this:

> "I was watching in the night visions,
> And behold, One like the Son of Man,
> Coming with the clouds of heaven!
> He came to the Ancient of Days,
> And they brought Him near before Him.
> Then to Him was given dominion and glory and a kingdom,
> That all peoples, nations, and languages should serve Him.
> His dominion is an everlasting dominion,
> Which shall not pass away,
> And His kingdom the one
> Which shall not be destroyed" (Daniel 7:13, 14).

The Ancient of Days, now with "the Son of Man"—a term used over and over in the New Testament by Jesus to refer to Himself (Matthew 17:22; 20:18; 24:30; Mark 2:10; 10:33; Luke 6:22; 11:30; 12:10; 17:22; John 6:53; 12:34; 13:31)—in some sort of heavenly event, another depiction of the judgment that leads directly to God's eternal kingdom.

Another picture of this same judgment, though first talking about events on the earth here, reads: "until the Ancient of Days came, and a judgment was made in favor of the saints of the Most High, and the time came for the saints to possess the kingdom" (Daniel 7:22; see also verses 26, 27). Notice: judgment made in *favor of God's people*. We tend to think of judgment as something bad, something that leads to punishment, which in many cases is true. But in this case, at least for the "saints" (a biblical term for God's people that has nothing to do with the Roman Catholic "sainthood"), judgment is made in their behalf.

How could that be, though? Have we not all been deemed sinners? Have we not already been told about how bad we are?

> " 'There is none who understands;
> There is none who seeks after God.
> They have all turned aside;
> They have together become unprofitable;
> There is none who does good, no, not one.'
> 'Their throat is an open tomb;
> With their tongues they have practiced deceit';
> 'The poison of asps is under their lips';

'Whose mouth is full of cursing and bitterness.'
'Their feet are swift to shed blood;
Destruction and misery are in their ways;
And the way of peace they have not known.'
'There is no fear of God before their eyes'"(Romans 3:11-18).

How, then, would any of us, even the "saints" in judgment, with the books opened, be able to stand before God, who, again, knows our every wrong thought, our every hidden deed, every single thing that we might have done in secret, things that we'd never want revealed (see Ecclesiastes 12:14)?

The everlasting gospel. That's how.

The Gospel and Judgment

It's no coincidence that the gospel and judgment appear together. However good the news of the gospel, it doesn't get any better than when linked with judgment. Why? Because our only hope in judgment *is the gospel*, is Christ's righteousness, which is accepted by the Father as our own the moment that we claim it by faith—and also in the judgment, *when we need it the most*. "There is therefore now no condemnation to those who are in Christ Jesus" (Romans 8:1). No condemnation now and certainly not in the judgment.

Is it because we are sinless? No, it's because Jesus was, and His record is credited to us as our own. That's why the judgment in Daniel 7 "was made in favor of the saints" (Daniel 7:22). They, like the thief on the cross, were covered by the righteousness of Christ. Or as Paul has said: "Therefore we conclude that a man is justified by faith apart from the deeds of the law" (Romans 3:28).

Justified apart from the law? Of course. The law, however "holy and just and good" (Romans 7:12)—a truth that becomes powerfully apparent in the third angel's message—points out sin but cannot atone for it. The law is like a mirror: it will keep your blemishes before you, but no matter how long and often you look into it, the mirror won't take those blemishes away. The law reveals sin; it offers no power to overcome or to forgive it. That's why we need the gospel.

One grand expression of the law and God's judgment came from the Old Testament sanctuary (and later the temple in Jerusalem), the center of worship for ancient Israel. This is the same temple that Jesus famously purged of those who had defiled the sacred grounds with their wanton and exploitative commerce (see Matthew 21:12, 13). It was here that the children of Israel learned about the plan of salvation, the "everlasting gospel." Central to the sanctuary service were the sacrifices of the animals, the lambs, bulls, goats—each one a symbol, a type, a mini-prophecy of Jesus' death on the cross, as well as His work as our high priest in the heavenly sanctuary (see below). That's why, when first introducing Jesus, John the Baptist cried out, "Behold! The Lamb of God who takes away the sin of the world!" (John 1:29). Instead of the sinner dying for his or her sin, the lamb, a symbol of Jesus, died in the sinner's place. Instead of us, ultimately, dying for our sins, Jesus on the cross did it for us. And this great truth had been proclaimed, in symbols and types, through the Hebrew temple.

The temple also had two apartments, and though every day the atoning blood of the animal sacrifices had been brought into the first apartment once a year (see Leviticus 16), the blood of animal sacrifices was brought into the second apartment, the inner compartment, in a ritual known as Yom Kippur, the Day of Atonement. This was the day of judgment, good news for the children of Israel, because even though they had sinned, their sin was forgiven, purged and cleansed by the shed blood, and they stood righteous before God in this judgment. This yearly ritual occurred "because of the uncleanness of the children of Israel, and because of their transgressions, for all their sins" (Leviticus 16:16). That is, they had sinned, and that was the day of reckoning for those sins.

However, that day was Yom Kippur, the Day of Atonement, and atonement is about forgiving sinners, not condemning them, and that forgiveness comes only from the blood—not from the law. Though in the second apartment of the sanctuary in the ark of the covenant (see Numbers 10:33; Deuteronomy 10:3; 31:26) were the stone tablets, the Ten Commandments, which showed Israel their sacred obligation to keep the law, atonement came about, not because of the law, but despite it. The law, which they had violated ("because of the uncleanness of the children of Israel, and because of their transgressions, for all their sins"), would have condemned them but for the blood. "He [the high priest] shall take some of the *blood* of the bull and sprinkle it with his finger on the mercy seat on the east side; and before the mercy seat he shall sprinkle some of the *blood* with his finger seven times. Then he shall kill the goat of the sin offering, which is for the people, bring its *blood* inside the veil, do with that blood as he did with the *blood* of the bull, and sprinkle it on the mercy seat and before the mercy seat" (Leviticus 16:14, 15). The mercy seat is the golden lid that covered the ark of the covenant, which contained the Ten Commandments, and the sprinkled blood on that mercy seat symbolized the blood of Jesus, which atoned for their violation of the Ten Commandments.

"This shall be a statute forever for you: In the seventh month, on the tenth day of the month, you shall afflict your souls, and do no work at all, whether a native of your own country or a stranger who dwells among you. For on that day the priest shall make atonement for you, to cleanse you, that you may be clean from all your sins before the Lord" (verse 29). This was a solemn day, the day of judgment, and the people were "to afflict their souls." That is, it was a day of repentance, of soul searching, of realizing their shortcomings, and, while depending upon the blood to forgive their sins, they needed the blood to cleanse them from those sins as well.

From the death of the animal to the priest ministering the blood in the sanctuary, everything prefigured "the everlasting gospel" (Revelation 14:6), with Jesus, first as the sacrifice, then as the high priest. An entire book of the New Testament, the book of Hebrews, explicitly explained that the earthly sanctuary was a model, a symbol, of the heavenly sanctuary, where Jesus, having shed His blood on the cross (symbolized by the animal sacrifices), now ministers in the heavenly sanctuary as our high priest.

"Now this is the main point of the things we are saying: We have such a High Priest, who is seated at the right hand of the throne of the Majesty in the heavens, a Minister of the sanctuary and of the true tabernacle which the Lord erected, and not man" (Hebrews 8:1, 2).

And just as the earthly priest interceded for the sinners by bringing the blood into the sanctuary, Jesus as our high priest in the heavenly sanctuary intercedes for us as well. "Who is he who condemns? It is Christ who died, and furthermore is also risen, who is even at the right hand of God, who also makes intercession for us" (Romans 8:34). "Therefore He is also able to save to the uttermost those who come to God through Him, since He always lives to make intercession for them" (Hebrews 7:25). "My little children, these things I write to you, so that you may not sin. And if anyone sins, we have an Advocate with the Father, Jesus Christ the righteous" (1 John 2:1). "For Christ has not entered the holy places made with hands, which are copies of the true, but into heaven itself, now to appear in the presence of God for us" (Hebrews 9:24).

Notice the theme here: Christ is in heaven, in the heavenly sanctuary, interceding *for us*. He is in the presence of God *for us*. He is an advocate *for us*. Which is why, now, in the time of this judgment ("for the hour of his judgment has come"), we have the assurance of salvation because of what Christ has done for us on the cross, as our sacrifice, and what He does for us now, in the heavenly sanctuary, as our high priest. Again: "Who is he who condemns? It is Christ who died, and furthermore is also risen, who is even at the right hand of God, who also makes intercession for us" (Romans 8:34), and because of that intercession for us, "there is therefore now no condemnation to those who are in Christ Jesus" (verse 1)—no condemnation now and, certainly, not in judgment.

In fact, the first angel's message about judgment occurs in the context of the Day of Atonement. Though the book of Revelation is filled with images from the earthly sanctuary (Revelation 1:20; 5:5; 8:3-8; 11:19; 15:5-8; 21:1-8), not too long before the events depicted in the three angels' messages unfold, Revelation 11:19 declares: "Then the temple of God was opened in heaven, and the ark of His covenant was seen in His temple." The temple is the sanctuary, and the ark of the covenant, in the second apartment, contained the Ten Commandments—and the only time the high priest entered the second apartment was on the Day of Atonement, the day of judgment.

Thus, what the first angel's message tells us is that, yes, "the hour of His judgment has come," which is why, though His people need to "fear God and give glory to Him," they do so with the assurance of "eternal life" in Jesus, promised them by the "everlasting gospel"—the promise that is theirs by faith.

How else?

Which Came First, the Grapefruit Seed, the Grapefruit, or the Grapefruit Tree?

It's a big universe out there. Two trillion galaxies with 100 billion stars each, and some of those stars have planets orbiting them, just as our sun does. Suppose on one of those planets the inhabitants got their nutrition, not from food, but from merely staring at their sun. A swami here on earth claims that we can do the same: get all our nutrition from the sun alone (though we advise not to try this at home).

Suppose that the beings on this planet were told about another planet, called Earth, where the inhabitants put pellets, little white pellets, in dirt, and that was it: They just left these little white pellets in dirt, and with only water and sunshine, out of these pellets grew trunks of wood, called trees, with dozens of branches. And on each of these branches sprouted green leaves from which coated packages of food—tasty, beautiful, nutritious food called "grapefruit"—would be created in abundance. And this is how the people on Earth got, at least partially, what they needed to survive. Suppose those people from this other planet were told, too, that inside those grapefruits many more white pellets would grow, and each single pellet could be taken out of the grapefruit and put into the dirt, and yes, more grapefruit trees would grow out of that one pellet in the dirt, creating more grapefruits that contain more pellets, and on and on infinitely.

Why would they believe it? Why *should* they believe it? Why would anyone believe it? Nothing is logical, nothing is commonsensical, and nothing is rational about a little white pellet containing even one grapefruit tree, much less potentially an infinite number of grapefruit trees, in itself. Just add dirt, water, and sunshine—and voilà, a grapefruit tree!

Please! If we had never seen anything like a seed in dirt turn into a tree filled with fruit bearing more seeds, why would we believe it? "They talked," wrote G. K. Chesterton of intellectuals, "as if the fact that a tree bears fruit were just as *necessary* as the fact that two and one trees make three. But it is not."*

No, it's not *necessary* at all. It is, instead, a miracle. But the only reason that we don't think so is that we see it happen all the time. But if only once in our entire lives we saw someone put a white pellet in dirt and out of that pellet came a grapefruit tree, we would deem it a miracle filled with awe and mystery.

And that's just the grapefruit. What about peaches, plums, apples, avocados, broccoli, lemons, tomatoes, coconuts, wheat, barley, rice, kiwi, cucumbers, apricots, bananas, blueberries, breadfruit, cherries, asparagus, cauliflower, celery, corn, eggplant, kale, onions, garlic, mustard, red pepper, radishes, blackberries, cantaloupes, watermelons, clementines, figs, olives, guava, mangoes, nectarines, passion fruit, spinach, strawberries, basil, mustard, okra, cranberries, and on and on and on? Each one of these arising from a pellet in the dirt? It's not logical, it's not rational, it's not sensible. It's, instead, a miracle. If only one time in our whole lives we can see any one of these alone (and this just what we can eat) arise out of the dirt, it would astonish us. But all of them? And every season, too? We're just so used to it that we don't see the miracle that it is.

Meanwhile, one might humbly ask: How did the grapefruit tree evolve? That is, how did it arise, unintentionally, with no thought at all going into it, as the theory of evolution speculates? (Evolution allows for no forethought, no intentions, no purposes, for any life forms on earth.) How does something that's only partially a grapefruit (or a cherry or a banana) seed, or partially a grapefruit (or a cherry or a banana) tree, or partially a grapefruit (or a cherry or a banana) evolve into a whole seed, a whole tree, or a whole grapefruit (or a whole cherry or a whole banana)? Or, instead, did one of them evolve first? If so, what came first: the grapefruit seed, the grapefruit tree, or the grapefruit? (It's a vegan version of the chicken-and-egg paradox: which came first, the chicken or the egg?)

However, the problem isn't really a problem, because the question itself—"What came first: the grapefruit seed, the grapefruit tree, or the grapefruit?"—is a false question. It assumes what it sets out to answer, which is that one of them, the tree, the seed, the fruit, had to come first.

But that's not what the Bible teaches. "Then God said, 'Let the land produce vegetation: seed-bearing plants and trees on the land that bear fruit with seed in it, according to their various kinds.' And it was so" (Genesis 1:11, NIV).

No one could answer which came first, because none did. According to the Bible, they were created at the same time, the only logical option to the dilemma. God created the grapefruit "with seed in it." And the same with peaches, plums, apples, avocados, broccoli, lemons, tomatoes, coconuts, wheat, barley, rice, kiwi, cucumbers, apricots, bananas, blueberries, breadfruit, cherries, asparagus, cauliflower, celery, corn, eggplant, kale, onions, garlic, mustard, red pepper, radishes, blackberries, cantaloupes, watermelons, clementines, figs, olives, guava, mangoes, nectarines, passion fruit, spinach, strawberries, basil, mustard, okra, cranberries, and on and on. Any one of these food sources, much more all of them together—beautiful, tasty, healthy, growing, literally, out of the dirt, should scream to us about our Creator God, a God who loves us.

Which leads, indeed, to what might be deemed the climax of the first angel's message. Yes, the first angel proclaims to us "the everlasting gospel." Yes, the first angel tells us to "fear God and give glory to Him, for the hour of His judgment has come." And finally, the first angel tells us to do one last thing: "Worship Him who made heaven and earth, the sea and springs of water" (Revelation 14:7).

What does this mean, to worship the Creator, the one who put the grapefruit tree in the seed, and the seed in the grapefruit tree—and why is it such an important message for us now?

Section Five

"For in Six Days . . ."

Read the first sentence of Scripture. It does not say, "For God so loved the world, that he gave his only begotten Son, that whosoever believeth in him should not perish, but have everlasting life" (John 3:16, KJV). It does not say, "But God commendeth his love toward us, in that, while we were yet sinners, Christ died for us" (Romans 5:8, KJV). It does not say, "Here is the patience of the saints: here are they that keep the commandments of God, and the faith of Jesus" (Revelation 14:12, KJV). The Bible does not open with the second coming of Jesus (Matthew 24:30). It does not open with human sinfulness (Romans 3:10), or with "the everlasting gospel" (Revelation 14:6), or with a warning about judgment (Ecclesiastes 12:14).

Instead, it opens with these words: "In the beginning God created the heavens and the earth" (Genesis 1:1). And that's because all these other teachings, the death of Jesus, the great controversy, human sinfulness, the fall of humanity, judgment—all these teachings make sense only if, yes, God created our world.

Otherwise, what? In a godless universe the death of Jesus on the cross would be just another murdered Jew. In a godless universe, what does the idea of final judgment mean? Who would do the judging? Or the rewarding? Or the punishing? In a godless universe, what could the "good news" possibly be other than that we live, we struggle, we suffer, we die—and then we are gone forever along with every memory of us. Some "good news," huh?

That's why the Bible begins with the truth upon which all other biblical truth—i.e., "the everlasting gospel," judgment, the great controversy, the Fall, everything that the Bible teaches—rests. And that is God as our Creator. Contrary to the modern idea that life here on earth arose by chance alone, with no forethought, no intention, no purpose, the Bible begins with what should be an obvious truth (again, think of the grapefruit): that life in all its beauty and stunning complexity was created by God.

And though the three angels' messages are specifically for the last days, the days that we are living in now, they point back to the first days, to the first *six* days, to the creation of life on earth itself. The language that John used in the first angel's message comes (as does much of Revelation) from the Old Testament. In this specific case the very wording of the angel's message—"worship Him who made heaven and earth, the sea and springs of water" (Revelation 14:7)—is derived from the fourth commandment, that is, the fourth of the 10, as in the *Ten Commandments*.

"Remember the Sabbath day, to keep it holy. Six days you shall labor and do all your work, but the seventh day is the Sabbath of the Lord your God. In it you shall do no work: you, nor your son, nor your daughter, nor your male servant, nor your female servant, nor your cattle, nor your stranger who is within your gates. For in six days the Lord made the heavens and the earth, the sea, and all that is in them, and rested the seventh day. Therefore the Lord blessed the Sabbath day and hallowed it" (Exodus 20:8-11).

Exodus 20:11 reads: "For in six days the Lord *made the heavens and the earth, the sea*"; the first angel's message reads: "Worship *Him who made heaven and earth, the sea*." Revelation 14:7 is a direct reference to the fourth commandment, which is itself a direct reference to the creation. The final words of the fourth commandment—"For in six days the Lord made heavens and the earth, the sea, and all that is in them, and rested on the seventh day. Therefore the Lord *blessed the Sabbath day and made it holy*" (Exodus 20:11, NIV)—come directly from the Genesis creation: "So *God blessed the seventh day and made it holy*, because on it God rested from all his work that he had done in creation" (Genesis 2:3, ESV).

The first angel (Revelation 14:6) takes us back to the fourth commandment (Exodus 20:8-11), which takes us back to the six days of Creation (Genesis 1-2). And embedded in the six days of Creation is the specific emphasis on the seventh day. "Thus the heavens and the earth, and all the host of them, were finished. And on the seventh day God ended His work which He had done, and He rested on the seventh day from all His work which He had done. Then God blessed the seventh day and sanctified it, because in it He rested from all His work which God had created and made" (Genesis 2:1-3).

A point worth remembering, too: When God blessed the seventh day, when He made it holy, and when He rested on it—only Adam and Eve existed. There were no Jews! The Jews didn't come into being until thousands of years later, after Abraham (see Genesis 29:35). The word "Jew" (or "Jews") first appears in 2 Kings 16:6 (KJV) and 25:25, in the context of invasions of the Hebrews in the eighth and sixth centuries B.C.—a long time *after* the Genesis creation account.

In other words, the idea, the common idea, that resting on the seventh-day Sabbath and keeping it holy is exclusively for the Jews is not biblical. Practicing Jews have been keeping the seventh-day Sabbath longer than anyone else, yes, and so they are commonly associated with it. But the seventh-day Sabbath didn't originate with, or from, the Jews any more than an apple, the ubiquitous logo for a computer company of that same name, began with Steve Jobs. The apple itself, like the seventh-day Sabbath, began in Eden, before the Jews and before Steve Jobs, no matter how much the seventh-day Sabbath is linked with the Jews, and the apple with Steve Jobs.

All through the Bible, Old Testament and New, the doctrine of creation appears. It's foundational to everything else because, again, everything else the Bible teaches means nothing apart from God as our Creator. That's why the theme appears again and again:

"By faith we understand that the worlds were framed by the word of God, so that the things which are seen were not made of things which are visible" (Hebrews 11:3).

"For thus says the Lord,
Who created the heavens,
Who is God,
Who formed the earth and made it,
Who has established it,
Who did not create it in vain,
Who formed it to be inhabited:
'I am the Lord, and there is no other'" (Isaiah 45:18).

"You are worthy, O Lord,

To receive glory and honor and power;

For You created all things,

And by Your will they exist and were created" (Revelation 4:11).

"In the beginning was the Word, and the Word was with God, and the Word was God. He was in the beginning with God. All things were made through Him, and without Him nothing was made that was made" (John 1:1-3).

"By the word of the Lord the heavens were made,

And all the host of them by the breath of His mouth" (Psalm 33:6).

"But ask the beasts, and they will teach you; the birds of the heavens, and they will tell you; or the bushes of the earth, and they will teach you; and the fish of the sea will declare to you. Who among all these does not know that the hand of the Lord has done this?" (Job 12:7-9, ESV).

"For this they willfully forget: that by the word of God the heavens were of old, and the earth standing out of water and in the water" (2 Peter 3:5).

"Thus says God the Lord,

Who created the heavens and stretched them out,

Who spread forth the earth and that which comes from it,

Who gives breath to the people on it,

And spirit to those who walk on it" (Isaiah 42:5).

"You alone are the Lord;

You have made heaven,

The heaven of heavens, with all their host,

The earth and everything on it,

The seas and all that is in them,

And You preserve them all.

The host of heaven worships You" (Nehemiah 9:6).

"For by Him all things were created that are in heaven and that are on earth, visible and invisible, whether thrones or dominions or principalities or powers. All things were created through Him and for Him. And He is before all things, and in Him all things consist" (Colossians 1:16, 17).

And there are many more texts that show just how important that doctrine of creation is. In fact, so important is the doctrine of creation, of God as the Creator, that we are *commanded* to spend one seventh of our lives, every week, without exception, to remember it—something that we are not commanded to do for any other doctrine. Why? Because, again, no other doctrine makes sense apart from God as our Creator. Right up there with "Thou shalt not kill" and "Thou shalt not commit adultery" and "Thou shalt not steal" is the commandment to "remember the Sabbath day." Why? Because "in six days the Lord made heaven and earth, the sea, and all that is in them." One seventh of our lives, every week, we are to remember, not the "deities" whom the pagans in antiquity worshipped, nor blind chance and natural selection, the deities of the modern secular world, but that God, and God alone, is the Creator.

How fascinating, too, that the first thing in the Bible declared holy is not a shrine, not a mountain, but a block of time—the seventh day. "Then God blessed the seventh day and sanctified it, because in it He rested from all His work which God had created and made" (Genesis 2:3). The word "sanctified" here is translated from a Hebrew word often meaning "holiness," and being "set apart for holy use." Though Creation dealt with the heavens, the earth, the birds, the beasts, and humans, things in space—it was time, not space, that God first pronounced blessed and holy. And that's because time is the dimension in which the things of space, i.e., the heavens, the earth, the birds, the beasts, humans, exist.

Finally, so important is this memorial to Creation that, instead of us going to it, the Sabbath comes to us. Once a week, at a thousand miles per hour (the approximate speed at which the earth rotates on its axis), the Sabbath circles the globe. "Arriving on one sundown, leaving on the next, the seventh day washes over the planet each week like a huge cleansing wave. We never have to seek it. The day always finds us."[1]

Here, then, in this warning message about the end of the world, the Word of God brings us back to the beginning of the world and, specifically, to the One who created it. And that is why we are told, not only to "fear" Him, and not only to "give glory" to Him, but also (and,

---

[1] Clifford Goldstein, *A Pause for Peace* (Nampa, Idaho: Pacific Press, 1992), p. 46.

perhaps, most important) to "worship" Him.

Worshipping the Image

A dramatic episode unfolds in Scripture. The choice is stark, clear, unambiguous. Obey the law of the land—or die. And die by being thrown alive into a burning furnace. No middle ground, no appeal, no pardon. Obey or burn.

But the issue is deeper: worship. Whom do we worship? Because, in the end, we all worship something. "In the day-to-day trenches of adult life," wrote American author David Foster Wallace, "there is no such thing as not worshipping. Everybody worships. The only choice we get is what to worship." [2] Self, fame, money, celebrities, sex, power—whatever. Worship isn't just about religious reverence or adoration or singing hymns of praise to the glory of the Lord. We worship whatever takes the place of God in our lives; whatever takes the place of God in our lives we worship. Atheists worship too.

The dramatic account is revealed in the Old Testament book of Daniel, a book that helps form a template, a background, to Revelation, where the three angels' messages are found. The episode unfolds in the ancient empire of Babylon, a name that, as we will see, plays a big role in the three angels' messages. Though the date isn't given, 594 B.C. or thereabouts is believed to be in the ballpark. The date isn't crucial; what happened is.

The empire of Babylon, under King Nebuchadnezzar, had conquered the nation of Judah, pillaging the land, destroying Jerusalem and its sacred temple, and carrying away captives. Among the captives were four young Jews whose Hebrew names were changed to Babylonian ones: Belteshazzar, Shadrach, Meshach, and Abed-Nego. Instead of laboring as slaves in some wretched mine or the like, these boys, of patrician Hebrew blood, were brought to the king's palace, where they, excelling in "all matters of wisdom and understanding about which the king examined them" (Daniel 1:20), served the king.

About this time, 594 B.C., King Nebuchadnezzar had a gold statue, a giant image, erected in his own honor, and then ordered everyone to worship the image. "To you it is commanded, O peoples, nations,

[2] https://web.ics.purdue.edu/~drkelly/DFWKenyonAddress2005.pdf

and languages, that at the time you hear the sound of the horn, flute, harp, lyre, and psaltery, in symphony with all kinds of music, you shall fall down and worship the gold image that King Nebuchadnezzar has set up; and whoever does not fall down and worship shall be cast immediately into the midst of a burning fiery furnace" (Daniel 3:4-6).

To obey this decree, however, would mean violating one of the Ten Commandments, the law of God. Old Testament, New Testament— the law of God is the standard of righteousness that God's people are called to obey. In the Old Testament, Moses tells God's people to "keep His commandments" (Deuteronomy 30:10); in the New, James writes: "For whoever shall keep the whole law, and yet stumble in one point, he is guilty of all. For He who said, 'Do not commit adultery,' also said, 'Do not murder.' Now if you do not commit adultery, but you do murder, you have become a transgressor of the law" (James 2:10, 11). Or, as expressed in Revelation: "Here is the patience of the saints; here are those who keep the commandments of God and the faith of Jesus" (Revelation 14:12).

And because one of the Ten Commandments says, "You shall not make for yourself a carved image—any likeness of anything that is in heaven above, or that is in the earth beneath, or that is in the water under the earth; you shall not bow down to them nor serve them" (Exodus 20:4, 5), these three men, Shadrach, Meshach, and Abed-Nego (Daniel—or Belteshazzar in Babylonian—was not in this story), refused to worship the image. They worshipped only the Creator, nothing or no one else. It was as simple as that.

Because of their refusal, they were hauled before the king, who asked: "Is it true, Shadrach, Meshach, and Abed-Nego, that you do not serve my gods or worship the gold image which I have set up?" (Daniel 3:14). Without much equivocation or double-talk, they replied, "O Nebuchadnezzar, we have no need to answer you in this matter. If that is the case, our God whom we serve is able to deliver us from the burning fiery furnace, and He will deliver us from your hand, O king. But if not, let it be known to you, O king, that we do not serve your gods, nor will we worship the gold image which you have set up" (verses 16-18).

Whatever historians know about ancient Near Eastern monarchs such as Nebuchadnezzar, they know that these men are not used to being talked to like that. Their response was not proper court etiquette. And, true to his word, he had the three of them thrown alive into a burning furnace. (Read Daniel 3 to find out how the story ended.)

The point here is—*worship*. Whom do we worship, for we all worship something. It is either the Lord—the one who "in six days . . . made the heavens and the earth, the sea, and all that is in them" (Exodus 20:11), and then "blessed the seventh day and sanctified it, because in it He rested from all His work which God had created and made" (Genesis 2:3)—or something else.

And to worship something else—anything else—other than the God who created us, who sustains us, the one in whom "we live and move and have our being" (Acts 17:28) and who ultimately redeemed us (the "everlasting gospel"), is idolatry. Whether worshipping the golden image, or science, or self, or money, or sex, or whatever we make into gods, it is still idolatry, because only the Lord has created us, only the Lord sustains us, only the Lord gives us life, and so only He, and He alone, deserves our worship. It's as simple as that.

One of the most famous works of art is the marble statue of King David, sculpted by Renaissance artist Michelangelo sometime between 1501 and 1504. Imagine standing before this block of marble, in the Accademia Gallery in Florence, Italy, and thanking it for being there, for being so exquisitely and finely detailed and crafted, even down to the veins in his hands, or for even existing, as if the statue had not only created itself but made itself into the stunningly beautiful work of art that it is. Instead of you praising and thanking Michelangelo, its creator, all your praise and honor is directed to the creation itself, as if it had created itself. Kind of nonsensical, is it not?

Though only analogous, this point about Michelangelo's *David* is what all idolatry, all false worship, is about: worshipping the creation, or some aspect of the creation (from self to statues to celebrities to science), as opposed to the Creator. As Paul expressed it: they "worshiped and served created things rather than the Creator—who is forever praised" (Romans 1:25, NIV). All through the Old Testament, God had warned against worshipping anything other than Himself. Whether the sun, moon, and stars (Deuteronomy 4:19), or the "gods" of the nations around them (Judges 10:6; Deuteronomy 8:19; 1 Kings 11:33; Psalm 81:9; Jeremiah 1:16), their idolatrous worship was futile and meaningless. Isaiah showed how futile it was:

> "He cuts down cedars for himself,
>> And takes the cypress and the oak;
>> He secures it for himself among the trees of the forest.
>> He plants a pine, and the rain nourishes it.
>> Then it shall be for a man to burn,
>> For he will take some of it and warm himself;
>> Yes, he kindles it and bakes bread;
>> Indeed he makes a god and worships it;
>> He makes it a carved image, and falls down to it.
> He burns half of it in the fire;
>> With this half he eats meat;
>> He roasts a roast, and is satisfied.
>> He even warms himself and says,
>> 'Ah! I am warm,
>> I have seen the fire.'
>> And the rest of it he makes into a god,
>> His carved image.
>> He falls down before it and worships it,
>> Prays to it and says,
>> 'Deliver me, for you are my god!'" (Isaiah 44:14-17).

In some cultures people are too sophisticated to do exactly what Isaiah warned about here. But the principle is the same: whatever takes the place of God in someone's life is false worship, and whatever it is, it can no more save them than Steve Jobs' computers or fame or money or power saved him. Sooner or later gravity is going put us all back in the dirt from which we first arose, and our only hope, our only salvation, is found in the Lord, in His "everlasting gospel." God alone deserves to be worshipped. Fame, sex, power, science, technology, self—none of these potential idols can save us any more than the carved image in Isaiah saved the one who carved it.

The episode of Shadrach, Meshach, and Abed-Nego and their refusal to worship the image is directly linked to the three angels' messages. In Daniel 3 the phrase "worship the gold image" appears six times (in verses 5, 7, 10, 12, 14, 18). The book of Revelation, in the chapter that leads up to three angels' messages, warns about a coming time of persecution. Under the threat of death, people will be forced to "worship the image" (Revelation 13:15). As in Daniel 3, the question of worship, and whom we worship, will become especially pertinent. The third angel's message itself, in fact, uses language from Daniel 3 when it too warns against worshipping this false "image" (Revelation 14:9, 11), which first appears in Revelation 13.

In summary, the first angel's message opens with the "everlasting gospel," the amazingly good news of Jesus, our Creator and our Redeemer, whose righteousness alone gives us hope in "the hour of His judgment." Besides calling us to "fear God and give glory to Him," the first angel's message climaxes, and ends, with a call to "worship Him who made heaven and earth, the sea and springs of water"—and who also established, in Eden, the seventh day as the memorial to that creation. This call to worship the Creator becomes, as we will see, more pointed when contrasted with the fierce warning in the third angel's message about worshipping "the image," at a time when the issue of worship will engulf the world.

We all worship. And, ultimately, we all worship one of two things: the creation or the Creator. One, the creation, this fallen creation, is what we need to be saved from; the other, the Creator, is the only one who can save us from it. Creation or Creator?

Whom do we worship?

One-Tongue World

It's a fascinating episode, one shrouded in the mysteries created by nothing but time because it unfolded deep in the past and our sole record, in Scripture, depicts it in only nine verses (Genesis 11:1-9). And yet its implications, its results, have reverberated through the millennia, to the very moment that you exist in now. The fact that you are reading these words in whatever language you are reading them—French, Spanish, Mandarin, Swahili, Hindi, Russian, whatever—is only because of what happened in this story. That's how basic, and consequential, the event was. Just as the seed in the grapefruit originated from Eden, different languages originated from the Tower of Babel.

The account opens with this line: "Now the whole earth had one language and one speech" (Genesis 11:1). Because all we have known, and for all recorded history too, is the reality of different languages (it's estimated that today about 7,000 different ones are spoken), the concept sounds strange, but, given that it was still relatively early in the history of the world, the idea of "one language and one speech" makes sense. "This is the book of the genealogy of Adam. In the day that God created man, He made him in the likeness of God. He created them male and female, and blessed them and called them Mankind in the day they were created" (Genesis 5:1, 2). One God, one race, one language.

Though the exact date of this account, the Tower of Babel, is unknown, the Genesis flood, the worldwide flood, had already happened. Noah died (Genesis 9:29), and his children and grandchildren and great-grandchildren multiplied and dispersed. (Genesis 10). Some dwelt in "a plain in the land of Shinar" (Genesis 11:2), the southern part of Mesopotamia, today's south Iraq. It was here that the people said long ago, "Come, let us build ourselves a city, and a tower whose top is in the heavens; let us make a name for ourselves, lest we be scattered abroad over the face of the whole earth" (verse 4). One could imagine, having heard about the Flood, these people seeking to protect themselves from another one, even though every rainbow painted across the sky was God's way of reminding them that "never again shall all flesh be cut off by the waters of the flood; never again shall there be a flood to destroy the earth" (Genesis 9:11). Thus, the building of a high tower whose "top is in the heavens" symbolizes defiance against God and His promises.

"Let us make a name for ourselves" depicts human arrogance and hubris as well. The word "name" there (in Hebrew, *shem*) appeared earlier in biblical history, when, before the Flood, in the context of how evil humanity was becoming, the Bible said: "Those were the mighty men who were of old, men of renown" (Genesis 6:4). "Renown" is a translation of *shem*, literally "men of the name." The next verse reads: "Then the Lord saw that the wickedness of man was great in the earth, and that every intent of the thoughts of his heart was only evil continually" (verse 5). Not long before the flood, and not long after, the idea of having a "name" (*shem*) depicts something negative.

The Tower of Babel narrative reinforces that unfortunate truth:

"And the Lord said, 'Indeed the people are one and they all have one language, and this is what they begin to do; now nothing that they propose to do will be withheld from them. Come, let Us go down and there confuse their language, that they may not understand one another's speech.' So the Lord scattered them abroad from there over the face of all the earth, and they ceased building the city" (Genesis 11:6-8).

Though details remain unknown, they were openly defying God, which is why He came down and confused their language. Imagine the bewilderment, the chaos, the confusion: hundreds, maybe thousands, of people, suddenly speaking to each other in languages that others didn't understand? They must have been astonished, fearful, angry, and frustrated all at once by something that they had never experienced before. It worked, too: they ceased; the city and the tower remained unfinished; and these confused people dispersed over the earth. Surely those who spoke a common tongue united with each other as they all spread out from Babel. We have here, then, the origins of different human languages.

The account ends with this verse: "Therefore its name is called Babel, because there the Lord confused the language of all the earth; and from there the Lord scattered them abroad over the face of all the earth" (verse 9). Babel, symbol of open rebellion and defiance against God, is the same word later used all through the Bible for "Babylon" (*babel* in Hebrew). The name "Babylon" appears hundreds of times in the Bible, from the days of the Judean monarchy, more than a half millennium before Christ, to the book of Revelation, where its first use is here: "And another angel followed, saying, 'Babylon is fallen, is fallen, that great city, because she has made all nations drink of the wine of the wrath of her fornication'" (Revelation 14:8).

Where is that? It's in the second angel's message. In fact, that is the second angel's message in entirety.

What is this message, and what does it say to us today?

Section Six

Babylon Is Fallen

The first angel's message is a proclamation about God: about His "everlasting gospel," about "His judgment," and about Him as Creator, the one "who made heaven and earth, the sea and springs of water." It's also about what our response to these great truths should be: fear, give glory to, and worship Him.

The second angel's message, in contrast, is not about God, not directly, but about an enemy of God (remember the great controversy). The message says: "And another angel followed, saying, 'Babylon is fallen, is fallen, that great city, because she has made all nations drink of the wine of the wrath of her fornication'" (Revelation 14:8). While we're at it—there's more in Revelation about Babylon, too. "'Babylon the great is fallen, is fallen, and has become a dwelling place of demons, a prison for every foul spirit, and a cage for every unclean and hated bird! For all the nations have drunk of the wine of the wrath of her fornication, the kings of the earth have committed fornication with her, and the merchants of the earth have become rich through the abundance of her luxury.' And I heard another voice from heaven saying, 'Come out of her, my people, lest you share in her sins, and lest you receive of her plagues. For her sins have reached to heaven, and God has remembered her iniquities'" (Revelation 18:2-5).

Ouch! Even before going to the Old Testament to learn what some of these images mean, the images themselves—i.e., "the dwelling place of demons," "the wine of her fornication," "a prison for every foul spirit," and "a cage for every unclean and hateful bird"—depict a spiritually unpleasant place for sure. However, there's also these other words, crucial words, from heaven: "Come out of her, my people." God has people, "my people," still there, though He tells them to get out before it's too late.

Babylon, Babel, even before the tower of that same name, symbolized opposition to God. In one biblical depiction of Satan—"O Lucifer, son of the morning! . . . For you have said in your heart: 'I will ascend into heaven, I will be like the Most High'" (Isaiah 14:12-14)—he is first referred to as "the king of Babylon" (verse 4), representing Babel itself.

In the Old Testament, Babylon had been a massive ancient empire. An enemy of God's people, Israel, Babylon had invaded and destroyed the nation. Many of the images in Revelation for this end-time Babylon have been taken directly from this same Old Testament Babylon:

Ancient Babylon	*End-Time Babylon*
1. This Great Babylon (Dan. 4:30)	1. Mystery, Babylon the Great (Rev. 17:5)
2. Babylon's harlotry (Eze. 23:17, 18)	2. The great harlot (Rev. 17:1)
3. Wild beasts in Babylon (Isa. 13:21)	3. Habitation of devils (Rev. 18:2)
4. Luxurious city (Isa. 13:19; Jer. 51:13)	4. Luxuriously adorned (Rev. 18:7)
5. Ruled the nations (Isa. 14:6)	5. Will reign over earth (Rev. 17:18)
6. Attacked Israel (Jer. 51:49)	6. Attacked God's people (Rev. 17:6; 18:24)
7. Nations drank of her wine (Jer. 51:7)	7. Nations drink of her wine (Rev. 14:8)
8. Use of sorcery and spells (Isa. 47:9, 12)	8. Works miracles (Rev. 16:14; 13:13, 14)
9. God's judgment against her (Jer. 25:28-30)	9. God's judgment against her (Rev. 18:8)
10. Nations against her (Jer. 51:27, 29)	10. Nations against her (Rev. 17:16)
11. Fall of Babylon (Isa. 21:9)	11. Babylon is fallen (Rev. 14:8)
12. Come out of her (Jer. 51:6, 45)	12. Come out of her (Rev. 18:4)

Long after the old empire of Babylon had been destroyed, the apostle Peter wrote: "She who is in Babylon, elect together with you, greets you; and so does Mark my son" (1 Peter 5:13). How could someone be in Babylon, which had vanished centuries earlier? Scholarship is certain that he's using this name as a symbol for the empire that had, by his time, replaced ancient Babylon as an opponent to God, which was Rome. This is the power that had crucified Christ (Mark 10:33; Matthew 20:19), that had persecuted the early church (see book of Acts), and that, unfortunately, continued that persecution in the papal phase, up to the early modern era (see Daniel 7:19-21, 24, 25; 8:10-12, 23-25).

The book of Daniel, in three prophetic chapters (Daniel 2; 7; 8), depicted a series of world empires. Two of these chapters, Daniel 2 and 7, started with Babylon (Daniel 2:36-38; 7:4), but then all three predicted the empires that followed—Media-Persia (Daniel 2:39; 7:5; 8:20), Greece (Daniel 2:32; 7:6; 8:21), and finally, Rome, which remains until the end of the world (see Daniel 2:33, 40-43; 7:7, 8, 19-27; 8:10-12, 23-25) and has a role to play in last-day events.

And, just as ancient Babylon, a vast religious and political power, opposed God and persecuted His people, modern Babylon is and does the same, only it will get worse as we near the end.

One of the images in the second angel's message is about Babylon's "fornication," an Old Testament image of unfaithfulness to God and His truth. The prophets used the idea of a pure woman, sometimes a bride, as a symbol of ancient Israel when it was faithful to God (Jeremiah 6:2). However, when it was unfaithful, when it went into apostasy, another image was used: harlotry. Ezekiel accused Jerusalem of playing the harlot "with the Egyptians," "with the Assyrians," "as far as . . . Chaldea" (see Ezekiel 16:26-29). "Have you seen what backsliding Israel has done? She has gone up on every high mountain and under every green tree, and there played the harlot" (Jeremiah 3:6). Thus, the image there of "fornication" gives the same idea: false doctrine, along with unfaithfulness to God and His truth that false doctrine inevitably brings.

Thus, the cry "Babylon is fallen" is another way of letting people know that the corrupt systems of this world will not win, will not dominate, regardless of how things seem now. Ancient Babylon, with its false teaching, errors, and persecutions, once seemed invincible. Modern Babylon might now too. But thanks to Jesus and His victory on the cross, sin, evil, Satan, the great controversy, and end-time Babylon, along with its false doctrines and teaching, will be forever gone, and this shout will be heard across the cosmos: "Alleluia! For the Lord God Omnipotent reigns! Let us be glad and rejoice and give Him glory, for the marriage of the Lamb has come, and His wife has made herself ready" (Revelation 19:6, 7).

The Third Angel

The third angel's message is a warning: "Then a third angel followed them, saying with a loud voice, 'If anyone worships the beast and his image, and receives his mark on his forehead or on his hand, he himself shall also drink of the wine of the wrath of God, which is poured out full strength into the cup of His indignation. He shall be tormented with fire and brimstone in the presence of the holy angels and in the presence of the Lamb. And the smoke of their torment ascends forever and ever; and they have no rest day or night, who worship the beast and his image, and whoever receives the mark of his name. Here is the patience of the saints; here are those who keep the commandments of God and the faith of Jesus" (Revelation 14:9-12).

Notice the imagery: straight from the book of Daniel, in which (see "Worshipping the Image") people were forced to "worship the . . . image" (Daniel 3:5, 7, 10, 14, 15, 18) on the pain of death. The warning in the third angel's message in Revelation 14 echoes Revelation 13 as well, in which people must, as in Daniel 3, worship an image or face death: "as many as would not worship the image of the beast to be killed" (Revelation 13:15).

Also, don't miss this point: the third angel's message comes right after—what? The proclamation of the second angel about *Babylon* being fallen (Revelation 14:8). What empire in the Old Testament forced the worship of an image? Babylon (Daniel 3:1).

Ancient Babylon, modern Babylon—the issue is worship.

The first angel's message calls people to worship the Creator, "who made heaven and earth, the sea and springs of water" (Revelation

14:7). This language comes directly from the Ten Commandments, specifically the fourth. "For in six days the Lord made heaven and earth, the sea, and all that is in them, and rested on the seventh day. Therefore the Lord *blessed the Sabbath day and made it holy*" (Exodus 20:11, ESV), which comes directly from the Genesis creation: "*So God blessed the seventh day and made it holy,* because on it God rested from all his work that he had done in creation" (Genesis 2:3, ESV).

The three angels' messages, then, present the great issue facing the world in the end-days: do we worship the Creator, or do we worship "the beast and his image" (Revelation 14:9)? The answer should be obvious: we worship God because He is the Creator, and there's no more foundational and basic symbol of Him as Creator than the seventh-day Sabbath, blessed and made holy in the first week, the Creation, and deemed by God important enough to be embedded in the Ten Commandments themselves!

This deep biblical truth, however, leads to an important question: Why, in most of the Christian world, is Sunday, the first day of the week, kept, as opposed to the seventh-day Sabbath, the biblical sign of God as Creator?

The following quotes explain why.

The 1977 edition of *The Convert's Catechism of Catholic Doctrine* reads:

"Q. Which is the Sabbath day?"

"A. Saturday is the Sabbath day."

"Q: Why do we observe Sunday instead of Saturday?"

"A. We observe Sunday instead of Saturday because the Catholic Church transferred the solemnity from Saturday to Sunday."—Peter Geiermann, *The Convert's Catechism of Catholic Doctrine* (Rockford, Illinois: Tan Books and Publishers, 1977), p. 50.

Rome admits to changing the foundational sign of God as our Creator to another day, Sunday? Here's another one:

"Q. How prove you that the church hath power to command feasts and holy days?"

"A. By the very act of changing the Sabbath into Sunday, which Protestants allow of; and therefore they fondly contradict themselves, by keeping Sunday strictly, and breaking most other feasts commanded by the same church."

"Q. How prove you that?"

"A. Because by keeping Sunday, they acknowledge the church's power to ordain feasts, and to command them under sin; and by not keeping the rest [of the feasts] by her commanded, they again deny, in fact, the same power."—Rev. Henry Tuberville, D.D. (R.C.) (1833), p. 58.

A human institution claiming to have changed God's law?

"Q. Has the [Catholic] church power to make any alterations in the commandments of God?"

"A. Instead of the seventh day, and other festivals appointed by the old law, the church has prescribed the Sundays and holy days to be set apart for God's worship; and these we are now obliged to keep in consequence of God's commandment, instead of the ancient Sabbath."—*The Catholic Christian Instructed in the Sacraments, Sacrifices, Ceremonies, and Observances of the Church by Way of Question and Answer,* RT Rev. Dr. Challoner, p. 204.

Here is one by a Roman Catholic luminary about the fact that the Bible never teaches that Sunday is the day of rest:

"Is not every Christian obliged to sanctify Sunday and to abstain on that day from unnecessary servile work? Is not the observance of this law among the most prominent of our sacred duties? But you may read the Bible from Genesis to Revelation, and you will not find a single line authorizing the sanctification of Sunday. The Scriptures enforce the religious observance of Saturday, a day which we never sanctify."—James Cardinal Gibbons, *The Faith of Our Fathers* (1917 edition), pp. 72, 73 (16th Edition, p. 111; 88th Edition, p. 89).

Google "Roman Catholic quotes about the change of the Sabbath," and you will find many more statements like these above in which Rome admits that Sundaykeeping is its, not God's, creation.

Some Protestants reluctantly admit that there's no biblical evidence for Sunday as opposed to the Sabbath. The leader of a Christian group in the United States dedicated to the observance of Sunday admitted just that. "There is," wrote James Westberry, "no record of a statement on the part of Jesus authorizing such a change, nor is there recorded a such a statement on the part of the apostles"

(James P. Westberry, "Are We Compromising Ourselves?" *Sunday,* April-June 1976, p. 5). Remember, these are the words from a man dedicated to keeping Sunday!

In *The Lord's Day,* a book dedicated to Sunday observance, Samuel Cartledge wrote: "We must admit that we can point to no direct command that we cease observing the seventh day and begin using the first day" (in James P. Westberry, ed., *The Lord's Day* [Nashville: Broadman Press, 1986], p. 100). They can point to no direct command because there is no command, direct or indirect, in the Bible to change the seventh-day Sabbath, instituted at Creation, to Sunday—a day that the Bible never treats as holy.

Are these Protestants saying, without coming right out and admitting it, that they have accepted Rome's change of the Sabbath, this foundational symbol, reaching back to Eden itself, of God as our Creator?

Seems so. Only it gets worse.

"Think to Change Times and Laws"

About 600 years before Christ, in the context of ancient Babylon, Daniel 2 (a prophecy parallel to Daniel 7) presented an amazing prediction that covered the history of the world from ancient Babylon down through our day, until God establishes His eternal kingdom. In the prophecy itself, after coming to the breakup of pagan Rome into the nations known today as modern Europe (depicted as kings), the text says: "And in the days of these kings the God of heaven will set up a kingdom which shall never be destroyed; and the kingdom shall not be left to other people; it shall break in pieces and consume all these kingdoms, and it shall stand forever" (Daniel 2:44).

Sometime, in the days of modern Europe, God will establish His kingdom. And this kingdom, which ends all earthly ones, will exist forever. And the great promise of the "everlasting gospel" is that by faith in Jesus, we all can have our place in it. "In My Father's house are many mansions; if it were not so, I would have told you. I go to prepare a place for you. And if I go and prepare a place for you, I will come again and receive you to Myself; that where I am, there you may be also" (John 14:2, 3). All that can keep us out is our own wrong choices.

The prophecy of Daniel 2, in summary, goes like this:

Babylon
Media-Persia
Greece
Rome
God's eternal kingdom (where Jesus has prepared a "place" for us)

As shown already (see "The Hour of His Judgment"), in Daniel 7 this same sequence of empires was also prophesized:

Babylon
Media-Persia
Greece
Rome
God's eternal kingdom (where Jesus has prepared a "place" for us)

In both prophecies the final earthly kingdom, the one that arises after ancient Greece and remains until God establishes His "kingdom which shall never be destroyed" (Daniel 2:44)—is Rome. Though pagan Rome vanished 1,500 years ago, papal Rome remains—and will continue to until God's kingdom at the end of this world.

Daniel 7, using different images, gave more details about these kingdoms than did Daniel 2, particularly regarding the last one, Rome, and particularly its papal phase, which included some unfortunate history, such as—it "shall persecute the saints of the Most High" (Daniel 7:25). Then, in the same verse about papal Rome's persecution of God's people, the prophecy also predicted that Rome would "think to change times and laws" (Daniel 7:25, KJV). Considering the quotes just looked at (see "The Third Angel"), in which Rome claimed to have established Sundaykeeping—a day that both Protestants and Catholics admitted has no scriptural backing—this verse is significant.

Notice: this verse says that it will "*think* to change times and laws." God's law, including the fourth commandment, was written in stone by the finger of God Himself. "Then the Lord delivered to me two tablets of stone written with the finger of God, and on them were all the words which the Lord had spoken to you on the mountain from the midst of the fire in the day of the assembly" (Deuteronomy 9:10;

see also Exodus 31:18). No earthly power can change that! The New International Version reads that Rome will "try to change" times and the law. *Trying* is not the same as *doing* it!

Jesus' death on the cross, for sin, which is defined as "the transgression of the law" (1 John 3:4, KJV), proves the immutability of God's law. Would not it have been better to have changed the law—or, to use an English expression, "to change the goalposts in the middle of the game"—in order to meet us in our sins so that Jesus would not have had to die for them (see 1 Corinthians 15:3)? Of course. Merely because someone claims to have changed the Sabbath day, and merely because most people follow the "changed" day, no more makes the Sabbath Sunday than someone's claim to have changed the law of gravity means that things will, now, fall slower to the ground, even if most people are under the delusion that they do.

This attempted change becomes of momentous importance when all the world will worship the beast—"as many as would not worship the image of the beast to be killed" (Revelation 13:15)—a worship that the third angel's message specifically warns against (Revelation 14:9-11). Or they will "worship Him who made heaven and earth, the sea and springs of water" (verse 7), an act memorialized in Eden in the seventh day—"God blessed the seventh day and made it holy, because on it he rested from all the work of creating that he had done" (Genesis 2:3, NIV)—and then immortalized in the fourth commandment: "For in six days the Lord made the heavens and the earth, the sea, and all that is in them, but he rested on the seventh day. Therefore the Lord blessed the Sabbath day and made it holy" (Exodus 20:11, NIV).

Worship the image? Worship the Creator? One or the other. That will be the choice before the whole world.

The Mark of the Beast

Revelation 13 repeats a great deal of imagery directly from Daniel 7, including Rome's past persecution of God's people—it "shall persecute the saints" (Daniel 7:25); it will "make war with the saints" (Revelation 13:7). The same verse that depicts this persecution, Daniel 7:25, also tells of Rome's attempt to change the law (it shall "think to change times and laws" [KJV]). Then, in the context of Rome (remember, in Daniel

2 and Daniel 7, Rome is the final earthly power remaining until God establishes His eternal kingdom), which is identified in Revelation 13:1-9 as a beast, the issue of worshipping the image in the last days first appears in Revelation 13:8, 12-15. This, in contrast to the three angels' messages, which warn against worshipping "the beast and his image" (Revelation 14:9, 10), but not before calling people to "worship Him who made heaven and earth, the sea and springs of water" (verse 7)—language taken from the fourth commandment, which the beast power had attempted to change!

To repeat: "A. We observe Sunday instead of Saturday because the Catholic Church transferred the solemnity from Saturday to Sunday" (Peter Geiermann, *The Convert's Catechism of Catholic Doctrine* [Rockford, Ill.: Tan Books and Publishers, 1977], p. 50).

The issue becomes clearer because, right after warning about this false worship, the third angel's message portrays God's people like this: "Here is the patience of the saints; here are those who keep the commandments of God and the faith of Jesus" (Revelation 14:12). In direct contrast to those who worship the beast and its image, God's people are depicted, besides having "the faith of Jesus," as keeping the commandments of God, which includes the one commandment that points to Him as the Creator, as the one "who made heaven and earth, the sea and springs of water" (verse 7)—again, the commandment that Rome had attempted to change!

Worship the Creator? Or worship the beast and its image? Can the issue of worshipping the beast and its image, or worshipping the Creator, Jesus (see John 1:1-3; Hebrews 1:1, 2; 1 Corinthians 8:6; Colossians 1:15-17), really be outwardly manifested over Sabbath versus Sunday?

How else? We worship God because, as the Creator (and also our Redeemer), He alone is worthy of worship (Revelation 5:9), and no more foundational symbol of Him as our Creator exists than the seventh-day Sabbath—blessed and made holy in Creation itself. For an earthly power, then, to seek to change, to usurp, the most basic sign, the seventh-day Sabbath, of the most basic doctrine, creation, is to attempt to usurp the Lord's authority at the most basic level possible: Him as Creator. The only level more basic is God Himself. No power, in heaven or on earth, can get to Him, so instead they get as close as possible: to the foundational sign of Him as Creator.

How fundamental is worship of the Creator to Christianity? It's a truth so fundamental that God commands one seventh of our lives, every week, to remember it. That's why it's hard to see how the controversy about worship—either worship of the beast (the very power that attempted to change the Sabbath) and its image, or worship of the Creator—could be centered on anything else but the day God established as a memorial to Him as Creator. This in contrast to the day that the beast power has established instead.

But killing people over the seventh-day Sabbath? Can that really happen? It already has! The Gospels themselves give us a precursor to it: those promoting human tradition wanting to kill because of the seventh-day Sabbath.

In John 9 Jesus had healed on the Sabbath a man blind from birth, perhaps the greatest miracle ever yet seen. "Since the world began it has been unheard of that anyone opened the eyes of one who was born blind" (John 9:32). How did the religious authorities respond? They accused Jesus of having violated the seventh-day Sabbath, saying, "This Man is not from God, because He does not keep the Sabbath" (verse 16). A conflict between human tradition (nothing in the Bible forbade healing on the Sabbath, just as nothing in the Bible has Sunday as a holy day) and God's law—specifically the seventh-day Sabbath of the fourth commandment—was brewing.

"Now when He had departed from there, He went into their synagogue. And behold, there was a man who had a withered hand. And they asked Him, saying, 'Is it lawful to heal on the Sabbath?'— that they might accuse Him. Then He said to them, 'What man is there among you who has one sheep, and if it falls into a pit on the Sabbath, will not lay hold of it and lift it out? Of how much more value then is a man than a sheep? Therefore it is lawful to do good on the Sabbath.' Then He said to the man, 'Stretch out your hand.' And he stretched it out, and it was restored as whole as the other" (Matthew 12:9-13).

How did the religious leaders respond to this astonishing expression of God's power? "But the Pharisees went out and plotted how they might kill Jesus" (verse 14, NIV).

Kill Jesus? Death because of the seventh-day Sabbath?

In John 5:1-16, after another miraculous healing on the seventh-day Sabbath, the religious leaders "persecuted Jesus, and sought to kill him, because He had done this on the Sabbath."

Wanting to kill because of the seventh-day Sabbath? Death because of human tradition versus the seventh-day Sabbath? Exactly! Though the specific issue here isn't the same as what the world will face in the final days, it's close enough: human law versus God's, and in these cases the part of God's law under contention is the Sabbath commandment, the one commandment that gets to the foundation of why we should worship only God, the Creator, and nothing or no one else.

In the life of Jesus, then, we can find precursors, hints, to what those "who keep the commandments of God and the faith of Jesus" (Revelation 14:12) will face: human tradition in conflict with God's law.

How does this idea, that of the mark of the beast centering on the biblical Sabbath, the seventh day of the week, versus human tradition, the first day, fit with the warning about the end-time power that "causes all, both small and great, rich and poor, free and slave, to receive a mark on their right hand or on their foreheads, and that no one may buy or sell except one who has the mark or the name of the beast, or the number of his name" (Revelation 13:16, 17)?

During the centuries, speculation has arisen over what the "mark on the right hand or their foreheads" means. But that's only what it has been, speculation. More remains to be revealed. But, going on the principle that the Old Testament holds the key to interpreting Revelation, we can find indications of what Revelation is talking about here.

Before the children of Israel were about to enter the Promised Land, Moses, having warned them many times about false worship, reminded them to keep God's commandments, that is, His law. He then said: "Therefore you shall lay up these words of mine in your heart and in your soul, and bind them as a sign on your hand, and they shall be as frontlets between your eyes" (Deuteronomy 11:18).

Exactly how they were supposed to bind his words to their hands and between their eyes, we don't know (the practice today of religious Jews "wrapping tefillin" is one interpretation). Yet they were to keep these words, God's law, "in your heart and in your soul," and this faithful adherence to God's law was to be manifested by the words being put on their hand, symbolic of deeds, actions, and on their heads, symbolic of their knowledge of God's law. Though one can't be too dogmatic about exactly how this was done in ancient Israel, or how in the last days this "mark on their right hand or on their foreheads" will be manifested either, there will be, it seems, some outward sign that will distinguish those who worship the beast and his image from those who, instead, "keep the commandments of God and the faith of Jesus" (Revelation 14:12).

(Also, for the record: only when the issues unfold in the last days does the mark come into effect. So, no—people who now keep Sunday do not now have "the mark of the beast.")

Finally, a question: How could something like this happen? An answer: We don't know. Though Revelation tells us *what* will happen, it does not tell us *how*. If, however, the COVID-19 pandemic has taught us anything, it's that our world, the entire world, can change—dramatically, quickly, dangerously. If in early 2019 people would have been told what we all would be doing in 2020 (lockdowns, quarantines, face masks, a pandemic with millions infected), most would not have believed it. After COVID-19 we should be aware that anything, even the unexpected (or, maybe, especially the unexpected), can happen, including, as the third angel warns, "the mark of the beast."

The Patience of the Saints

The first angel's message begins with the "everlasting gospel" (Revelation 14:6); the third angel's ends with it: "Here is the patience of the saints; here are those who keep the commandments of God and the faith of Jesus" (verse 12). Faith ("the faith of Jesus") and obedience ("keep the commandments of God")—if that's not the gospel, the "everlasting gospel," what is?

Debate exists on the precise meaning of "the faith of Jesus." Is it the faith of Jesus, in that it reflects the faith that Jesus had manifested when here; or is it the faith that believers have placed in Jesus? Either way, as the Bible says: "But that no one is justified by the law in the sight of God is evident, for 'the just shall live by faith'" (Galatians 3:11).

How else but by faith?

Considering that the power who created space, time, matter, and energy, that is, who created the universe itself, had "shrunk down," becoming one of us, and then offered Himself as a sacrifice for our sins—*we are going to add to that?* As if the death of the Creator were, somehow, not enough to pay for our sins? No matter how bad you might have been, the sacrifice of Him who "is before all things, and in Him all things consist" (Colossians 1:17) certainly was more than enough to cover you. And by faith, "the faith of Jesus" (however we understand it), you can claim His death in your behalf, right now, and stand perfect before your Creator as if you had never sinned.

And "the commandments of God"? Which commandments? At last count, there were 10. The book of Revelation, besides Revelation 14:12, makes references to them. Just before the vision that includes the three angels' messages, Revelation 11:19 reads: "Then the temple of God was opened in heaven, and the ark of His covenant was seen in His temple." The "ark of His covenant" is the place where the Ten Commandments were stored in the earthly sanctuary.

Specific commandments also appear in Revelation. The first angel's message, to worship God (Revelation 14:7), directly refers to the first commandment (Exodus 20:1-3), and (as we have seen) this same message uses language directly from the fourth. The third angel warns against worshipping the image (the image of the beast), which points to the second commandment, against idolatry (Exodus 20:4-6). Meanwhile murder, theft, and adultery are all covered in Revelation 9:20, 21 alone. Revelation 12:17, the final verse before Revelation 13, where the mark of the beast is introduced, depicts God's people: "And the dragon was enraged with the woman, and he went to make war with the rest of her offspring, who keep the commandments of God and have the testimony of Jesus Christ." Twice (Revelation 12:17; 14:12), then, in the context of last days, God's faithful people are depicted as keeping His commandments.

And why not?

A man went to his 30-year high school reunion. After he left, thinking about how messed up so many of his old friends were, one thought entered his mind: *If only people had kept the Ten Commandments—how much better their lives would have been!* Imagine our world if everyone kept even just some. If no one violated the sixth commandment (murder), the seventh (adultery), the eighth (thievery), and the ninth (lying), our existence would be paradise compared to what it is now.

A thought experiment: what country would you rather live in and raise a family? A country in which everyone obeyed the Ten Commandments, or in which no one did? The answer alone reveals how beneficial "the commandments of God" are for us.

And the good news of the "everlasting gospel" is that the same faith, "the faith of Jesus," that takes hold of Christ's righteousness, which covers our sin, is the same faith that takes hold of Christ's righteousness, which also cleanses our sins and transforms us. "If anyone is in Christ, he is a new creation; old things have passed away; behold, all things have become new" (2 Corinthians 5:17).

We are promised, over and over, the power to obey, to overcome, and to keep God's commandments.

"No temptation has overtaken you except such as is common to man; but God is faithful, who will not allow you to be tempted beyond what you are able, but with the temptation will also make the way of escape, that you may be able to bear it" (1 Corinthians 10:13).

"For everyone who has been born of God overcomes the world. And this is the victory that has overcome the world—our faith" (1 John 5:4, ESV).

"I can do all things through Christ who strengthens me" (Philippians 4:13).

"We know that our old self was crucified with him in order that the body of sin might be brought to nothing, so that we would no longer be enslaved to sin" (Romans 6:6, ESV).

"Now unto him that is able to keep you from falling, and to present you faultless before the presence of his glory with exceeding joy" (Jude 24, KJV).

Yes, we can, by God's grace, keep His commandments, even perfectly. We just can't keep them perfectly enough to be saved by them. That's why salvation is by faith, and not by the law. We are "justified by faith without the deeds of the law" (Romans 3:28, KJV) because the deeds of the law cannot justify us. If they could, why didn't Jesus skip the cross? Why didn't He just come to the earth, show us how to obey,

95

and then return to heaven? It was because, as much as we needed an example, we needed a substitute as well, which is why He died on the cross, suffering in Himself the penalty for our having already broken God's law. "But God demonstrates His own love toward us, in that while we were still sinners, Christ died for us" (Romans 5:8). The cross alone shows the futility of human works for salvation.

And we need to be saved, don't we? Please! As bad as this world has been, it's going to get worse. Daniel warns of "a time of trouble, such as never was since there was a nation, even to that time" (Daniel 12:1). However, even though at first things will get worse, they will get better—better beyond anything that we could imagine. "For behold, I create new heavens and a new earth; and the former shall not be remembered or come to mind" (Isaiah 65:17). "Nevertheless we, according to His promise, look for new heavens and a new earth in which righteousness dwells" (2 Peter 3:13). "Now I saw a new heaven and a new earth, for the first heaven and the first earth had passed away" (Revelation 21:1). "And God will wipe away every tear from their eyes; there shall be no more death, nor sorrow, nor crying. There shall be no more pain, for the former things have passed away" (verse 4).

No more death? No more sorrow? No more pain? It's an existence that we, who have known only death, only sorrow, only pain, cannot envision. These "former things," which never should have been here to begin with, will pass away, and a new existence will be ours forever. That's what the "everlasting gospel," formulated "before time began" (2 Timothy 1:9), promises. This new existence is what the three angels' messages are, ultimately, pointing to. It's what the prophets dreamed about, had visions about, preached and wrote about. And it's what, ultimately, Jesus died for. "He shall see the labor of His soul, and be satisfied" (Isaiah 53:11). And living in the times that we do, we can be the people of the prophet's dreams, we who, by faith, the "faith of Jesus," will one day proclaim:

"Behold, this is our God;
　　We have waited for Him, and He will save us.
　　This is the Lord;
　　We have waited for Him;
　　We will be glad and rejoice in His salvation" (Isaiah 25:9).